Packard

Dennis Adler
Foreword by Jay Leno

MBI Publishing Company

Dedication

For Jeanne, my constant companion and eternal inspiration. To Don Sommer and David Holls for their invaluable help and friendship over the years, and in memory of one of the great automotive designers of the twentieth century, my friend, *Franklin Q. Hershey.*

First published in 1998 by MBI Publishing Company, 729 Prospect Avenue, PO Box 1, Osceola, WI 54020-0001 USA

MBI Publishing Company books are also available at discounts in bulk quantity for industrial or sales-promotional use. For details write to Special Sales Manager at Motorbooks International Wholesalers & Distributors, 729 Prospect Avenue, PO Box 1, Osceola, WI 54020-0001 USA.

Library of Congress Cataloging-in-Publication Data

Alder, Dennis.
    Packard / Dennis Adler.
      p.   cm.
    Includes index.
    ISBN 0-7603-0482-3 (alk. paper)
    1. Packard automobile--History. I. Title.
TL215.P25A35   1998
629.222--dc21   98-8464

Edited by Keith C. Mathiowetz
Designed by Katie L. Sonmor

On the front cover: Owned by actor/producer Robert Achor, this 1932 Packard 903 DeLuxe Eight convertible sedan was the 45th of the type 533 models built on the short 142 1/2-inch wheelbase chassis. In 1932, Packard offered 10 body styles for the 903 DeLuxe Eight and this was the most expensive, priced at $4,550.

On the frontispiece: Packards carried several different ornaments through the years, but the "Goddess of Speed" was probably the most famous. Between 1926 and 1950, this popular mascot appeared in many forms, but it always remained recognizable. Here the goddess adorns the radiator of a 1930 Packard Model 745 with a custom body by Letourneur et Marchand.

On the title page: The 1934 LeBaron 1106 speedsters were built in very limited numbers. Of the handful produced, one was ordered by Douglas Fairbanks and another by Carol Lombard as a gift to Clark Gable. The cars sold for $7,745, making them among the most expensive Packard models of the early 1930s.

On the back cover: From beginning to end, Packard created only quality, prestigious automobiles. From the top are a 1910 Model Eighteen five-passenger touring, a 1934 Model 1108 Custom Dietrich convertible victoria, and a 1953 Caribbean.

Printed in Hong Kong through World Print, Ltd.

Contents

Acknowledgments

So many people become involved in the creation of an automotive book—historians, designers, collectors, and restorers—that it becomes a collective effort, more than the work of a single individual.

Packard owners are among the most dedicated car collectors in the world: enthusiasts with a will not only to preserve the cars, but to preserve the history of the company as well.

In the creation of *Packard*, our personal thanks and gratitude go out to a handful of individuals who contributed to this book in countless ways. Russ Murphy, adjunct curator, automotive history, Detroit Historical Museums, who provided a wealth of historical photos never before published; Mark Patrick, curator, Detroit Public Library National Automotive History Collection; Don Sommer, a life-long Packard enthusiast whose knowledge of the company provided invaluable insight; David Holls, retired General Motors vice president of design, who allowed us access to his personal photo archives of Packard custom coachwork and to the history of his late friend Howard "Dutch" Darrin; Dr. Joseph A. Murphy, whose collection of rare Packards comprises a good portion of the new color photography in this book; Bill Snyder, collector and historian; Robert Turnquist, author, collector, restorer, and the dean of Packard authorities; long-time collector and restorer Jerry Sauls; Otis Chandler, who has owned some of the greatest Packards ever built; Jerry J. Moore, who never fails to bring the best of the best to America's leading Concours d'Elegance; and the many Packard owners who contributed their time in the creation of this book.

To each and all, my sincerest thanks and appreciation. Without you, this book could never have been done.
Dennis Adler

Foreword

When Dennis Adler asked me to write the foreword for his new book, I thought to myself, "What can I say about Packards that everyone doesn't already know?" The history of this great American auto company is legendary, so my thoughts are perhaps on a more personal level, as a Packard owner and an automotive enthusiast.

I'm probably the archetypal car nut because I'm much more comfortable with car people I can learn things from than guys who just want to show off what they've got. So I hang out with guys where I'm sort of the dumbest one around, which actually isn't that hard to do, because there are huge, gaping holes in my knowledge. The guys I really like are engineers and machinists. Once I get with people who really know what they're talking about, I realize, "Oh man, I don't know anything at all."

Old cars are very complicated, and you really learn to appreciate the engineering. That's why I've always had a fondness and respect for Packards. The very first American classic I ever bought was a Packard Twin Six. They were probably the most mechanically sound cars of their time.

As an enthusiast, the cars that most attract me are orphans, cars built by companies that are now defunct or out of business. What that means to me is the people were more engineers than businessmen, and consequently, they refused to make compromises, and they paid for it by going out of business. For the greatest part of its history, Packard was very much an uncompromising company, building big, extremely powerful, and tastefully styled cars throughout the 1920s and 1930s. That's when a car, at least to me, really defined the national character. The Packard Twin Six and Packard Twelve, as prime examples, were the finest cars that Packard Motor Company ever produced and probably the best built cars in the world at the time.

My attraction to Packards really goes back to my childhood. Not that I'm that old. I grew up in the 1950s, so my interests in cars should be grounded in an entirely different era, but I had older parents. When I was born, my dad was 42, my mother was 41, and my brother was already 10, so my points of reference as a kid were always the Depression and earlier because that's what my father talked about. He wouldn't say "refrigerator"; he would say "icebox"; he wouldn't say "record player"; he'd say "Victrola." So when my dad talked about a car, it would be something no one had heard of. He'd say something like, "the REO, there was a truck," and as a kid, you know, you always want the stuff your folks talk about. I remember him telling stories about going somewhere and saying, "Oh, this Packard went by, and it was as long as a city block, and it was shiny black . . . ," and in my mind I thought, well, that's the car to have. Why would you want a 1950s car when you could get yourself a Packard, because that's what would impress my father. So maybe the cars I like are more a reflection of my dad.

People are always asking me why I like old cars so much, and I think one of the reasons is that you have to be more involved with an older car than a new one. To me to fuss around with it for a half hour before I get in and go is as much fun as getting in it and going. I enjoy changing spark plugs, and I enjoy checking carburetor balance, just doing all the things I need to do to make it right. To me it makes you more of an enthusiast. You have to be what they called back in the old days an "automobilist." In the 1920s and 1930s you had to be serious to own one of these cars. You had to know how to take care of it. You had to risk breaking down because having the car was worth whatever happened to it. As an enthusiast, there's a real sense of accomplishment when you get an old car running. That's a wonderful feeling.

In this book, Dennis Adler brings back many of those wonderful feelings through his original color photography of more than 50 great Packard models produced from the early 1900s to the 1950s, along with over 125 vintage black and white photographs from Packard's six decades in the automobile trade. This is a welcomed addition to the telling of the Packard story.

*I*ntroduction

PACKARD—AMERICA'S MOST COLLECTIBLE CLASSIC

Considering that thousands of automotive names have come and gone since the turn of the century some 98 years ago, and that a good many of them were American makes—Duryea, Winton, Pope-Hartford, White, Peerless, and DuPont—to name just a few, it seems remarkable that any one marque could have become so singularly popular today as Packard. The Packard name is acknowledged in every automotive circle, whether it is among members of the Antique Automobile Club of America, the Classic Car Club of America, or any of the countless postwar-era car clubs that gather from coast to coast. No matter what the period, from the days of the horseless carriage to the fabulous fifties, there is a Packard model for every automotive interest.

Along with V-12 and V-16 Cadillacs, Chrysler Imperials, and KB Lincolns, Packard Eights and Twelves were judged among the most prestigious luxury cars in the world, particularly in Europe where Packard was revered as the best American car built. Packard's early success as an auto maker allowed the firm to put more cars on the road than any other independent manufacturer, and throughout the greatest era in the history of the automobile, the 1930s, no auto maker except for Cadillac offered as wide a variety of models. Packard seemed invincible, and for the longest time it was.

The demise of once-great marques, like Marmon, Pierce-Arrow, Franklin, Auburn, Cord, and Duesenberg, can be explained for the most part by the harrowing economics of the Depression era, yet Packard survived the worst period in American automotive history, contributed to the war effort, remained profitable, and in the late 1940s was still regarded as highly by consumers as were Ford, General Motors, and Chrysler. Packard was so much a part of the American automotive scene from the turn of the century on, that it is often hard to believe the company could possibly have failed.

How popular are Packards today? All one needs to do to answer that question is look in the Classic Car Club of America directory and see that there are more Packards listed than any other make. Among them, the Packard two-door convertibles rank as the most desirable body style ever produced, followed closely by the convertible victoria, and then phaetons, but it is all a matter of personal preference. As to model years, cars produced from 1932 through 1934, in the opinion of most collectors, are the best of the best.

As collectors' cars, Packards are so numerous that they have never been overpriced by collectors and have held their value longer when it comes to appreciation and resale. Packards did not go up as high in price during the boom years of the late 1980s, as did models like the J and SJ Duesenberg. Consequently, they did not fall as far in value during the 1990s, or at all in some cases. There are, of course, some exceptions, such as one-off or very limited production models with full custom coachwork; but as a rule Packard prices are reasonable.

For many collectors, pursuing non-Classic models has proven to be an even more affordable alternative. The Packard One Ten and One Twenty series offered a number of very stylish cars with coachwork similar to the Senior models, but at a fraction of the price. An even more popular alternative is the prewar Packard Clipper. Ranked among the most advanced American cars on the road in 1941 and 1942, the Clippers represented a bold departure from Classic-era styling and traditional manufacturing techniques. Clippers are truly a class unto themselves, and the last great cars to bear the Packard name.

While collectors of the first new postwar Packards introduced in 1948 may disagree with that popular opinion, as will owners of the good-looking Caribbean models produced in the early 1950s, with only the heavy-handed Patrician designs and Caribbean, Packard was never able to reclaim its prewar distinction as a manufacturer of premium luxury automobiles. Faced with declining sales, bad investments, and the merger with Studebaker, Packard found itself on the brink of financial ruin in the early 1950s. Ironically, had the political and economic conditions that influenced the federal government's bailout of Chrysler in the 1970s occurred 20 years earlier, Packard would surely have survived its financial crisis, regained its stature, and developed an entirely new line of luxury cars in the late 1950s to rival any in its past. And it might well have been Packard, instead of Chrysler, that absorbed American Motors Corporation in the 1980s. This would have been a twist of fate more just than any in automotive history, since it was the creation of AMC that contributed to Packard's ultimate demise. But it was not to be, nor was Packard. While it is strictly conjecture among automotive enthusiasts and historians, Packard's fate was already sealed by 1956, its future guided by forces outside the company's control.

The Packard story is a six-decade-long odyssey that began in Warren, Ohio, and ended in a leased building on Conner Avenue in Detroit, Michigan. It is a reminder that giants fall and the best of intentions can lead to the worst imaginable consequences. It is life played out on the grandest scale and portrayed by the most omnipresent contraption that man has ever created, the automobile.

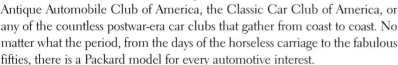

At the high end of the Packard scale are cars like this 1934 LeBaron Model 1108 V-12 dual-cowl sport phaeton, the most valuable and luxurious models ever to bear the Packard name.

OPPOSITE

An affordable Classic, the 1942 Packard Super Eight Custom One-Eighty Clipper touring sedan was on the cutting edge of American automotive technology at the outbreak of World War II.

One

The Customer Is Always Right

THE EARLY PACKARD MODELS

James Ward Packard was not an auto maker. In fact, he was barely an automotive enthusiast in the late 1890s. Then again, how many people were? The horseless carriage was a fanciful idea, and everyone with a notion of how to couple an internal combustion engine to a surrey was trying to emulate the success of J. Frank Duryea, the man who first put America on motor-driven wheels in 1896. One of Duryea's most notable followers was Alexander Winton who had emigrated to the United States from Scotland in 1884, first establishing a bicycle manufacturing business in Cleveland, Ohio, in 1891, and then venturing into the motor carriage trade in 1897 with the Winton Motor Carriage Company.

Following contemporary motor carriage design using chain drive and tiller steering, Winton placed his engine in the rear of what for all intents and purposes was a two-seat, four- to six-passenger wagon (one bench seat facing forward, another aft of the engine compartment, facing rear). Winton, however, built his motorcar with exceptional durability and powered the earliest model with a 10-horsepower twin that propelled the carriage to a then breathtaking speed of 33.64 miles per hour. In another two-cylinder model, Winton

drove from Cleveland to New York City, a feat that earned him headlines in the *Cleveland Plain Dealer* and clinched the sale of his first car on March 24, 1898. Within a year, Winton had built and sold more than 100 automobiles, one of which was delivered to James Ward Packard early in 1898. Unfortunately, this car was fraught with mechanical problems from the start, and Packard ended up having it towed home by a team of horses after it broke down on the last leg of his trip back from Cleveland. Packard found it necessary to make several trips to Cleveland, speaking with Winton himself, who at first was eager to make whatever repairs were needed. The car, however, was continually plagued with breakdowns, and by the end of the year Packard was thoroughly disgusted. He had also come to know Winton and his chief engineer, George Weiss, on a first-name basis.

Packard was trying to be a gentleman when he very politely told Winton that he had found some faults with the automobile. Mr. Packard then suggested to Mr. Winton that he make some minor changes to the car's design, incorporating certain more or less novel ideas of his own. What

---

The Model A was Packard's first production motor carriage. This example, completed in Warren, Ohio, on November 6, 1899, was used for an early publicity photo. Cataloged as a 2-P roadster, the 71 1/2-inch-wheelbase channel-iron chassis was fitted with coachwork manufactured in Warren by carriage makers Morgan and Williams. The body construction was wood with a black varnish finish. Seat upholstery was top-grade leather. The Packard chassis used two back-to-back half-elliptic leaf springs, mounted transversely for the suspension, and two full elliptic leaf springs in the rear mounted between the axle and body. *National Automotive History Collection, Detroit Public Library*

OPPOSITE

The first Packard motor carriage, manufactured in 1899 at Packard Electric in Warren, Ohio. It was powered by a single-cylinder engine developing 9 horsepower at 800 rpm. The engine used suction intake, mechanical exhaust valves, and had a fixed head cast in one piece. Bore and stroke was 5 1/2x6 inches for a swept volume of 142.6 cubic inches. The transmission provided two forward speeds through a center chain drive. *National Automotive History Collection, Detroit Public Library*

This is the second Packard automobile produced and was, for about a year, the personal conveyance of William Doud Packard (pictured behind the shovel handle tiller), who is said to have driven the car as far as Lakewood, New York. Somewhat different in design from the first Model A, this example had a larger dash panel with a storage compartment for tools and packages. The storage compartment also had a cushioned top so that two additional passengers could perch rather precariously facing rearward, surrounded on three sides by only a narrow brass rail. This design gave real meaning to the expression "back seat driver." The body for this example was produced for Packard by Morgan and Williams Buggy Manufacturers, in Warren, Ohio. *National Automotive History Collection, Detroit Public Library*

happened next was an argument printed in the press two years later by journalist Hugh Dolnar of *Cycle & Automobile Trade Journal*, in which he reported the Cleveland, Ohio, auto maker's reply to Mr. Packard: ". . . the Winton waggon [sic] as it stood was the ripened and perfected product of many years of lofty thought, aided by mechanical skill of the highest grade, and could not be improved in any detail, and that if Mr. Packard wanted any of his own cats and dogs worked into a waggon [sic], he had better build it himself, as he, Winton, would not stultify himself by any departure whatever from his own incontestably superior productions."[1] This was likely the first recorded case of poor customer relations in the American automotive industry.

Interestingly enough, Dolnar's telling of this story accompanied a review of the 1901 Packard automobiles being produced in Warren, Ohio. It was the third year of production for James Ward and William Doud Packard, who had decided to take Alexander Winton's advice.

The Packard brothers were already highly successful manufacturers of incandescent lamps and electrical transformers, a flourishing enterprise in

turn-of-the-century America where the Edison electric light was far more practical than a motorized carriage, but the Packards saw great promise in the horseless carriage and, being financially and technically capable of pursuing this new endeavor, proceeded to build an automobile that met up to *their* expectations, going into competition with Winton and a handful of other upstart auto makers.

Scions of a wealthy family whose roots in this country dated back to the seventeenth century, the brothers' father, Warren Packard, and the Packard family had established businesses in both Pennsylvania and Ohio and owned one of the most successful hardware stores in the East and interests in iron and lumber mills. Packard also played a significant role in supplying materials for building the Atlantic and Great Western Railroad. Thus James and William had the luxury of growing up in one of early America's more affluent families, attending the best schools, and following the careers that most interested them.

William graduated from Ohio State University in 1882 and pursued a variety of positions within his father's companies. James attended Lehigh University in Bethlehem, Pennsylvania, and graduated in 1884 with a degree in mechanical engineering. Unlike his brother, James chose to make his way outside the family business, joining the Sawyer-Mann Electric Company in New York City. The young Packard quickly advanced from a superintendent with Sawyer-Mann to foreman of the firm's mechanical department, where he developed and patented a magnetic circuit and an incandescent lamp bulb, a design that was later sold to Westinghouse.

In 1890, James left Sawyer-Mann and with his brother, William, formed the Packard Electric Company in Warren, Ohio. Packard Electric was a progressive and highly innovative company that ultimately became one of the largest automotive wiring suppliers in the United States, and in the early 1930s, one of many acquisitions of the expanding General Motors empire. Of course, by then Packard Electric was no longer involved with the Packard Motor Company, which had grown into one of the most successful independent automotive manufacturers in the country, and in the luxury car field, a staunch competitor to GM's Cadillac division. Back in the late 1890s, however, the automobile had been just a gleam in James Ward Packard's eye, a reflection of

In 1901 Packard offered two models, the 9-horsepower Model B and the new 12-horsepower Model C, pictured outside the Warren, Ohio, factory. The new model featured such controversial devices as a steering wheel, highly debated at the time as being more difficult to control than the previous tiller-type steering spoke. The Model C developed a standard output of 12 horsepower at 850 rpm, from a single-cylinder engine of 183.8 cubic inches. Bore and stroke was now a nearly square 6x6 1/2 inches. Body types included the 2-P roadster shown, roadster with high rear passenger seat facing forward, and 4-P surrey. The price of a new Packard in 1901 was $1,500. An optional folding top was an additional $50 to $75. *National Automotive History Collection, Detroit Public Library*

An assembly line of sorts, this picture of the Packard factory in Warren, Ohio, was taken in the spring of 1903 as the new Model F went into production. An improved version of the first Model F introduced in November 1901, both versions were the first Packards to use a two-cylinder engine. Output was 24 horsepower delivered via a three-speed sliding gear transmission and chain drive. *National Automotive History Collection, Detroit Public Library*

*I*n 1946, in preparation of Packard's 50th anniversary celebration, members of the East Grand Boulevard shop restored a 1901 Model C roadster equipped with the high rear passenger seat. The car was used in a Packard promotional campaign and in 50th anniversary parades. *Department of Automotive History, Detroit Historical Museums*

the new Winton he had recently purchased and with which he had quickly become disenchanted.

Taking Winton at his word, Packard's first car, the Model A, was introduced in 1899. By 1900 he not only had refined the earlier design and introduced the Model B, but he hired away two of Winton's engineers, including his top man, George Weiss. Weiss joined the Packard brothers in establishing their first automotive manufacturing enterprise, Packard and Weiss, which officially became the "Automobile Department of The New York and Ohio Company, a division of Packard Electric." That year Packard sold 49 cars, including 2 to William D. Rockefeller, a former owner of 5 Wintons!

With a taste of success, in August 1900, Packard and Weiss took the plunge and reorganized the auto-making concern into a separate business from New York and Ohio, forming the Ohio Automobile Company, with James as president of the board and general manager, William as treasurer, and Weiss as vice president.

In 1901 Packard had both the 9-horsepower Model B and new 12-horsepower Model C in production.[2] The company's first magazine advertisement featuring "The Packard Automobile" and Packard's now-famous "Ask the Man Who Owns One" slogan appeared in the October 31, 1901, issue of *Motor Age*.

Five weeks earlier, Packard had entered three of his cars in an endurance run from New York City to Buffalo, sponsored by the Automobile Club of America. All three cars, the fastest of which was driven by James Packard and George Weiss, were among the first to finish the six-day tour, which was cut short on the final leg by tragic news of President McKinley's assassination at the Pan American Exposition.[3] Despite this dark moment in American history dashing the enthusiasm of everyone involved in the tour that was scheduled to end at the Pan American Exposition in Buffalo, Packard was pleased to claim second and third for top speed. Even with one car having been temporarily sidelined following an accident, all three Packards finished the grueling 390-mile endurance run, which claimed half of the 80 automobiles entered. It may well have been this achievement that led to the Packard slogan in 1901.

Packard's stellar year concluded with two new models being displayed in the first National Automobile Show held that November at Madison Square Garden in New York. By the spring of 1902, Packard was headed down the road to success, a road that would soon turn in a new direction: Detroit, Michigan.

Two

$\mathcal{E}$ast Grand Boulevard

THE MOVE FROM WARREN, OHIO, TO DETROIT, MICHIGAN

While James Ward Packard established the Ohio company bearing his name, the auto maker's early future was guided by Henry Joy, whose father, James F. Joy, played an integral role in governing the Michigan Central Railway and the Chicago, Burlington & Quincy Railroad. Like James Ward Packard, Henry Joy grew up in comfortable surroundings and attended the finest schools. And like Packard, he worked his way through the business world becoming president of the Fort Union Street Depot in 1900.

Joy's education was in the sciences, having attended the Sheffield Scientific Institute at Yale University in the late 1800s. Thus, his innate interest in all things mechanical was piqued when he saw Henry Ford's first efforts in 1898. Joy's fascination with the horseless carriage finally brought him to New York, where the finest selection of gasoline and steam-driven models could be found. It was on one such sojourn that he visited the Adams and McMurtry agency in New York City and saw his first Packard, a 1901 Model C. The rest, as it is so often said, is history.

Joy purchased the car from Adams and McMurtry and ordered a new 1902 Model F as well. It wasn't long before he had to meet the automobile's maker. Joy and Packard took an immediate liking to one another, and in short order Henry Joy was a stockholder in the Ohio Automobile

Company of Warren, with a substantial investment of $25,000. By the middle of 1902, Packard sales were increasing both in New York and at the new Packard distributorship in Chicago and Philadelphia.

Joy's involvement in the Ohio Automobile Company continued to grow, and in 1903, after the board of directors issued an additional 2,500 shares in the company, Joy and a group of Detroit investors purchased the entire offering. At that same meeting, the name of the company was officially changed to the Packard Motor Car Company. Thus was laid the groundwork for the move from Warren, Ohio, to Detroit.

Joy's investment group included such Detroit luminaries as dime store magnate John Newberry (who was Henry Joy's father-in-law); Truman H. Newberry; Joy's partner, financier Russell A. Alger Jr.; Fred M. Alger; Joy's brother Richard; C. A. DuCharme; D. M. Ferry Jr.; Joseph Boyer; and Phillip H. McMillan. Altogether Joy and his associates invested more than a quarter of a million dollars in Packard by 1903, and in so doing gained controlling interest of the company.

The decision to move operations to Detroit was made long before anyone in Warren was willing to concede that Packard had outgrown its Ohio-born roots. But the truth was, even if Packard hadn't run out of space

Created sometime in the mid-1930s, this composite photo was used to show the many sides of Packard, from engineering and manufacturing to testing. *Department of Automotive History, Detroit Historical Museums*

OPPOSITE

Taken in 1938, this photograph shows the Packard One Twenty plant, which was bordered by East Grand and Concord. *Department of Automotive History, Detroit Historical Museums*

to expand its operations, with controlling interest in the company seated in Detroit, the move would have come about regardless.

In Detroit, Joy commissioned architect Albert Kahn to draw up plans for an assembly plant and executive offices. (During his career, Kahn would go on to design many of the Ford, Chrysler, and General Motors assembly plants as well, making him the most renowned industrial designer in the automotive industry.) The site Joy chose for the new Packard factory was an open field occupied in 1903 by grazing cattle. It was on the outskirts of Detroit at the far end of what was then known as Grande Boulevard. The design of the original buildings also called for a spur to be built off the Michigan Central Railway, which would allow cars to be taken directly from the factory and loaded into railway cars for delivery to Packard's expanding tally of retailers.

The first Packard plant in Detroit opened its doors on September 22, 1903, just 90 days after ground was broken. Kahn's design for Packard was a watershed, the first structure of its type built to provide employees with a well-lighted working environ-

ment. The earliest buildings were built of conventional wood framing with a brick exterior, but the walls were lined with tall, double-hung windows which allowed light to pour over the work areas and give laborers a less confined feeling. The structural design of later buildings erected in 1905 employed Kahn's latest structural techniques, the use of reinforced concrete construction, pioneered by Albert's brother Julius Kahn. The 1905 Packard buildings and the revolutionary "Kahn system" launched an entire generation of new construction in Detroit. Packard, however, was the first, and in the early 1900s, what was later to become East Grand Boulevard stood as the most advanced factory in the world for automobile manufacturing.

Throughout the early years in Detroit, Packard's land holdings increased almost annually. Henry B. Joy's perpetual factory building program was commensurate with increasing sales and profits, and by the end of 1911, the plant had increased to 1,642,212 square feet covering 37.7 acres.

"Packard Factory Spreads In All Directions," wrote the *Automobile* in 1911. Continuing to sing the

*I*n one section of the East Grand plant, the Packard body shop crew assembled the frameworks for the cars. Wood was used extensively in the early years to create the skeleton to which steel and fabric were attached. *Department of Automotive History, Detroit Historical Museums*

praises of Packard, the article concluded, ". . . that when a company manufactures all of the parts of its cars itself, instead of merely assembling parts made elsewhere, it can turn over its capital approximately once during a fiscal year."[1] In 1912 Joy was pleased to show his investors the best year in Packard's history up to that time, profits of $1.8 million on sales of $14.6 million.

Packard was doing as well as any independent auto maker in the country, better than most, actually, and it was during the early 1900s that the cars from East Grand came to be known as one of the "Three Ps" in American luxury cars. The other two were Pierce-Arrow and Peerless. Together they became known as the three finest names in design, engineering, and style. Packard, however, was at the forefront as the American automotive industry approached the middle of the second decade.

At Packard's helm with Joy was Alvan Macauley, who joined the company in 1911 as general manager. With the addition of Jesse Vincent in 1912, the

triumvirate that would guide Packard for the remainder of the decade was in place.

Changes at East Grand came swiftly with Macauley directing operations and Vincent developing new engines and engineering for the cars. Packard had its new six-cylinder engine and traditional fours, and by 1915 would introduce the unprecedented 12-cylinder Twin Six, engineered by Vincent.

Packards were among the most carefully constructed and highly detailed cars built in America. The Packard process of painting the chassis and undercarriage provided the cars with an even more exclusive look. The coachwork was handcrafted in the body shops, and the wood framing and wood trim meticulously machined and finished in the wood shop. Packards leaving East Grand Boulevard were the epitome of handcrafted luxury. Regardless of the model, body style, or price, every Packard received the same level of craftsmanship. By the end of the decade, the assembly buildings covered more than 40 acres, and employment was at an all-time high for the era, with between 6,000 and 7,000 salaried workers.

During World War I, the Packard facilities produced thousands of Liberty aircraft engines and the Le Pere U.S. Army combat 11 aircraft, which unfortunately arrived too late to participate in the war. Packard had, however, entered the aviation age with

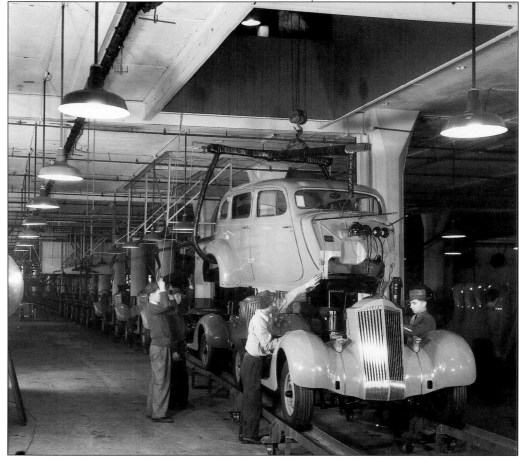

as much haste as GM, Ford, and others. The cost, not so much financial, was the complete disruption of the assembly lines. By the end of the war, Packard had built 6,500 Liberty aircraft engines.

In the years following World War I, East Grand continued to expand, outward and upward, adding stories to the original buildings. By the 1930s there was a massive bridge connecting the two main facilities facing the Boulevard.

The Packard factories were in their heyday during the 1930s. Bodies were built on the south side of the street and rolled across the enclosed bridge. With the exception of custom coachwork, the standard bodies were still being crafted in Packard's own shops, and when the semicustom lines were added in the late 1920s, coachwork was still finished in the Packard shops and the final assembly completed at East Grand.

The first major revision of the Packard assembly process, which was conducted on several floors, was the modernization of the plant in 1935 to begin construction of the One Twenty series.

Over the years, Detroit had grown up around Packard, which was now at the center of a thriving

*O*verhead track was used to move components around the chassis shop. It was here that every Packard had its beginnings, regardless of the coachbuilder. *Department of Automotive History, Detroit Historical Museums*

*C*harlie Vincent got to test Packards at the Proving Grounds after they were built; but in brother Jesse Vincent's engineering department, Packard engines, in this instance a Twelve, were fully inspected before moving on to the chassis mounting. *Department of Automotive History, Detroit Historical Museums*

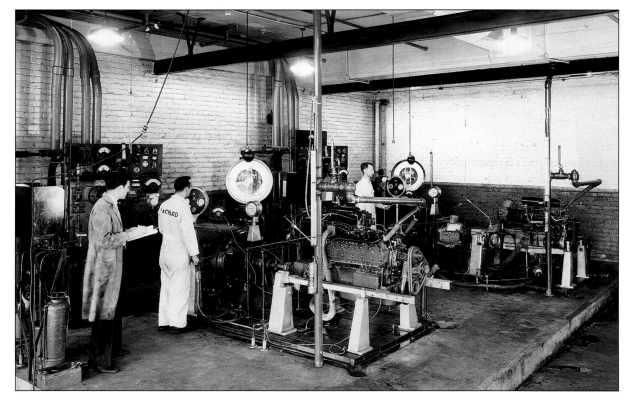

This was East Grand's own little torture test, the "Body Shaker" used to test chassis, suspension, and body fit. *Department of Automotive History, Detroit Historical Museums*

metropolis, a far cry from the days when Henry Joy purchased land surrounded by open fields and roaming livestock. In the middle of the Depression, there were surly times when everyone at East Grand longed for those simpler days; but with Packard's unrivaled success over the preceding 35 years came the responsibility of leadership.

Packard reached a crucial impasse, the size of its market was substantially reduced by the financial crisis blighting the American economy, and though the company was financially sound, it was posting annual losses. Thus, "Into [a] new and untried middle ground Packard cast its fortunes," the company said in 1935. Macauley summarized it by telling the Packard Board that in order for the company to remain competitive, it would have to build cars in more than one price range. It was, after a fashion, a reprise of the early teens, when Packard produced both a junior and senior line of cars—the Eighteen and the Thirty—which while sharing similar body styling, were separated by wheelbase, engine size, and performance. Thus in its past, Packard found the way to its future. East Grand set about creating a new kind of car, one

that would have to retain all of the marque's heralded qualities, but at a cost far less than any of its time. This was the challenge of the One Twenty.

To build such a car, Packard needed to redesign its assembly process and streamline the operation to higher efficiency. This task fell upon George T. Christopher, who was brought on board as an assistant vice president and production manager for the new venture. One entire section of the Packard facility had already been stripped bare with the consolidation of the Senior product line. Christopher had to use the available floor space and transform it into the One Twenty production department. This he did in a record 90 days, creating one of the industry's most efficiently mechanized assembly lines.

The One Twenty plant was a virtually self-contained operation producing its own engines, transmissions, and so on on the first floor, with coachwork completed one flight up in the body shop. The finished shells were then moved to the "body drop," an opening in the floor above the rolling chassis, one story below. Finished cars rolled out the end of the building with the punctuality of Fords. George Christopher's masterpiece, the

Four brand new 1935 Packard One Twenty sedans leave East Grand (in background) and head off to a local distributor. *Department of Automotive History, Detroit Historical Museums*

One Twenty, became the first mass-produced automobile in Packard history, and in all probability, the savior of the Packard Motor Car Company in the 1930s.

Prosperity returned to the Boulevard, and as the last years of the decade unfolded, Packard produced some of the finest cars in its history. Had it not been for the onset of a second world war, Packard would have steamrolled into the 1940s as one of the country's most popular and profitable auto makers. Fate, however, had a different future in store for the factories spanning East Grand Boulevard.

On February 9, 1942, George Christopher, along with factory managers and workers, rolled the last production Packard off the assembly line, above it a sign which read

Here's the last PACKARD
'Til we win the war.
It's "all out" on ENGINES
To even the score!

The East Grand Boulevard factories, converted to produce Merlin aircraft engines and Packard marine engines, became one of the largest independent military suppliers to the U.S. and British military during the war. As early as 1940, Packard had contracted to produce Rolls-Royce aircraft engines, and ground was already broken for three new buildings dedicated to the aviation field. When the United States entered the war, Packard devoted more than 1,000,000 square feet of floor space to military production. In the interim, of course, automobile manufacturing was pushed completely aside and the well-organized assembly lines at East Grand converted to the tasks at hand. The cost to Packard would ultimately be the very company itself. East Grand would never fully recover from the losses of the war—damage to tooling and the tremendous technical and material setbacks that would plague the company in the late 1940s.

Packard emerged from the war with its factories in shambles and the Utica Proving Grounds in ruins.

The company may have been financially sound, but as the 1950s approached, Packard's house was in need of a complete overhaul.

In the early part of 1941, in what had been deemed to be a cost-saving measure, Packard transferred body production to the Briggs Body Company. As a result, East Grand was no longer in the business of building Packard coachwork after the war. This was to become one of the company's greatest errors. What had first appeared to be an economical advantage would turn into a financial disaster by the early 1950s, and one of the weakest links in Packard's postwar recovery.

The East Grand facilities were no longer being used to their best advantage, and by 1955, a year before the fall of Packard, what had once been the paradigm of automotive manufacturing had turned into a pariah that Packard itself could no longer afford to maintain, and of which Studebaker had no need. By the end of 1956, nearly all of Packard's operations had moved from East Grand; the Packard Proving Grounds was closed down; and all that remained of a glorious past had come to an end without ceremony. In June 1956 the doors were closed at East Grand Boulevard. The entire complex, land and all, was sold for a mere $750,000 in 1957 by a struggling and near-bankrupt Studebaker-Packard. The property has since traded hands numerous times. Mostly in ruin today—its once tall windows broken out and busy alleyways strewn with refuse—the lower floors of the buildings are rented out for storage space, but for the most part, the Boulevard is a massive, empty shell of concrete, brick, and memories.

For those who still hold the Packard marque in highest esteem, it is also a monument to a time when East Grand was a center of commerce and Packard one of the greatest auto makers the world has ever known.

*T*hree

The First Great Packard Automobiles— 1904-1919

BUILDING AN AUTOMOTIVE EMPIRE

By the early 1900s, Packard and Winton were among the two most competitive auto makers in the country. In 1903, both had succeeded in completing transcontinental trips across the United States to prove the durability of their automobiles. To tell the truth, however, the majority of early Packards, Wintons, and every other car then built, were barely suitable to the roughhewn roadways of North America, if you could call them roads at all. Little had changed outside of the major cities since the Civil War.

Once outside the city limits, roadways were little more than graded dirt trails allowing motorcars to proceed no faster, and often with less success, than a horse-drawn carriage. In the early 1900s, more than one farmer made a day's wages with his plow horses by towing automobiles sunk to their hubs in mud, or extracting the cars of ashen-faced drivers from roadside ditches. Despite road conditions that were better fit for beast than manmade machines, throughout the first three years of production, Packard annually refined his designs, perhaps in mock defiance to Winton's vainglorious assertion that his cars ". . . could not be improved in any detail." Progressing through the Models A, B, C, F, G, and in 1903 introducing the Model K, Packard had finally established himself as one of the country's leading manufacturers, pioneering such features as automatic spark advance (which would not become an industry standard until years later) and the "H" pattern shift gate.

In 1904, a year after the company moved its manufacturing operations to East Grand Boulevard in Detroit, Packard introduced its first contemporary-styled motorcar, the Model L, and along with it the distinctively shaped Packard radiator shell that would become a trademark for decades.

Despite an image founded on building touring cars, Packard also built one of the first sporting automobiles in America, a model known as the run-about, or Gentleman's Roadster. The design was introduced in 1904 on the Model L, and by 1909 had been refined into a very swanky two-seater. Packard had also changed its system of identifying models from letters to numbers, which now indicated the actual horsepower output of a car, beginning in 1906 with the Model 24, the Model Thirty in 1908, and the lower-priced companion Model Eighteen in 1909. There was a quick switch to spelling the number after the first year. Packard continued to use this nomenclature up until 1913, when models were cataloged by engine and series.

The new 1909 Model Eighteen was the first attempt at producing a downsized Packard, although the company didn't consider it as such. The Eighteen wasn't even viewed as a new model line, rather a smaller Thirty, built to the same standards and quality ". . . for use in the city where the extra weight and power of the Thirty is not needed."

---

*T*he Packard driver had a lot to think about behind the wheel, with controls spread well apart and the three-speed gear change located on the outside of the driving compartment. The gas pedal was placed in the middle, between the clutch and brake.

OPPOSITE

*I*t was referred to as "a gentleman's car built by gentlemen." This 1909 Model Eighteen Gentleman's Roadster is a prime example of the luxurious styling that helped establish Packard in the early 1900s. This stunning all-white example from the collection of Dr. Joseph A. Murphy was photographed at the historic New Hope train station in New Hope, Pennsylvania.

Another Model Eighteen, this one produced in 1910 with a five-passenger touring body. Riding on tall 34x4-inch Firestone tires mounted on wood-spoke artillery wheels, this handsome model sold for $3,200. *Car courtesy of the Classic Car Club of America Museum. Photo by Dennis Adler*

A view from the driver's seat (all early Packards were right-hand-drive) shows the large wood-rimmed steering wheel, hand controls, floor pedals, and the optional speedometer, still a rare item on early automobiles.

The same body styles used on the Thirty were available for the Model Eighteen, although slightly redesigned to fit the car's nearly 1-foot-shorter 112-inch wheelbase. The Model Thirty had a 123 1/2-inch span between the axles.

Packard Eighteen prices ranged from $3,200 to $4,400, with the Model Thirty demanding from $4,200 to $5,750, depending upon the style of coachwork.

The sportiest of the Eighteens was the Gentleman's Roadster, such as the stunning all-white example pictured in this chapter from the collection of Dr. Joseph A. Murphy. White was among several special colors offered in 1908 as an alternative to the traditional Packard color scheme of Richelieu Blue with cream striping and running gear. Optional colors tacked on an additional $25 to the base price.

The runabout was produced on an even shorter 102-inch-wheelbase chassis, riding on 34-inch tires and powered by the standard 18-horsepower T-head four-cylinder engine. The price without options was $3,200, while the larger Model Thirty was $1,000 more with like body styling. The two-seat Model Eighteen was one of the first American cars to be considered *sporty*, and actually preceded such well-

A beautifully detailed engine, this is the Model Eighteen T-head with a 4 1/6x5 1/8-inch bore and stroke, displacing 326 cubic inches and delivering 18 horsepower at 650 rpm through a three-speed sliding gear transmission and expanding flywheel clutch. *Car courtesy of the Classic Car Club of America Museum. Photo by Dennis Adler*

known and popular raceabouts as the Mercer Model 35, Stutz Bearcat, and Oakland Speedster.

By the early 1900s, Packards were among the most expensive automobiles in America. Even as the less costly Model Eighteen Gentleman's Roadster was still pricey at more than $3,000. To put Packard in perspective, a Ford Model T runabout, a sort of spindly, unadorned rendition of the Gentleman's Roadster, sold for $825, and this at a time when Fords were still rather high-priced. Ford has always been something of an ersatz yardstick for comparing the values of luxury cars against those of corresponding

upholstered items were the seats) and was adorned throughout with polished brass trim, cowl lamps, headlights, radiator shell, and cap. (Chrome plating had yet to be created, and the only option to polished brass was nickel plating, a very costly process usually reserved for only the most expensive automobiles such as Rolls-Royce.)

The Packard motorist had a full complement of gauges on the Model Eighteen, including a speedometer, a feature that was still relatively new. On the Model Eighteen, the brass-cased drum-type gauge was mounted just forward of the three-speed gear change, located on the outside of the driving compartment. The pedal arrangements followed European design, with the throttle—a flat pedal at the base of the steering column—flanked on the right by the brake pedal and the clutch on the left.

The Packard Model Eighteen engine was a four-cylinder T-head design with a 4 1/6x5 1/8-inch bore and stroke, displacing 326 cubic inches and delivering 18 horsepower at 650 rpm through a three-speed sliding gear transmission and expanding flywheel clutch. It wasn't exactly breathtaking performance, but underway, speeds approaching almost 60 miles per hour *were* breathtaking, since there was no windshield or oval steering-column-

*F*ollowing Packard's move to Detroit in 1903, the new factory was built on East Grand Boulevard. With the Packard office building as a backdrop, Packard test driver Edward F. Roberts and company director Sidney Waldon posed with the first Model L built at the new Detroit plant. Waldon was another of Packard's most celebrated test drivers and publisher of Packard's first periodicals, *Strong Talk*, *Packard Pointers*, and *The Packard* magazine. *National Automotive History Collection, Detroit Public Library*

*R*eady for a dealer-promoted outing, Packard owners line up in front of the Willis-Haywood-Holcomb Company dealership in Indiana. Pictured from left are a 1908 Packard Thirty runabout with rumble seat and two 1909 Thirty seven-passenger touring cars. Both touring models were fitted with the folding cape top. Note the massive center headlight mounted on a stanchion in front of the radiator cap on the first seven-passenger tourer. *National Automotive History Collection, Detroit Public Library*

everyman's models, and the difference in price continued to expand as time went on. By 1915, Ford would drop the average cost of its cars to under $500, while Packard's would exceed $5,000.

The Gentleman's Roadster was handsomely upholstered in leather (at this point in time the only

Very formal livery in the guise of a 1909 Packard Model Eighteen "NA" landaulet. The carriage-like coachwork featured an open chauffeur's compartment, solid central roof section, and folding rear top. The Model Eighteen was built on a 112-inch-wheelbase chassis. The Model Eighteen was also offered in an imperial limousine version suggestive of early 1900s Edwardian styling. *National Automotive History Collection, Detroit Public Library*

Behind the wheel of Packard's sportiest model for 1912, the Packard Six runabout, is Packard company director Henry Joy, who was instrumental in bringing Packard to Detroit in 1903. As a rather substantial investor, Joy had also been responsible for the company's name change on October 13, 1903, to the Packard Motor Car Company. As the largest stockholder outside of the Packard brothers and George Weiss, Joy and his Detroit associates eventually gained majority control of the company, steering Packard anew in the early 1900s. *National Automotive History Collection, Detroit Public Library*

During the early 1900s, Packard had also delved quite successfully into the manufacturing of truck chassis. Pictured is a rather handsome 1910 panel delivery, this example used by the Packard Motor Car Company. *National Automotive History Collection, Detroit Public Library*

One of the largest chassis produced is this 1917 E Series commercial, used by Hampden Transfer Company of Baltimore. The idea of building commercial trucks had been that of Packard president Henry B. Joy, who recognized the need for commercial vehicles as far back as 1903, when as a major stockholder, he suggested to James Ward Packard that the company build a truck on the Model F chassis. That was the beginning of an entire line of Packard trucks suitable to every need. By 1917, Packard was also providing trucks for the American military. Packard commercial chassis were used for supply and troop transport trucks during World War I. *National Automotive History Collection, Detroit Public Library*

mounted wind pane for the driver. Driving goggles were a must, as were hat and duster—proper accouterments for motoring circa 1909. By the end of its first decade, Packard was considered among the most prestigious automotive marques in the world. A Packard ad in the September 16, 1911, *Saturday Evening Post* made note that 14 percent of all parties registering at the swank Elton Hotel in Water-

bury, Connecticut, were driving Packards—twice as many as any other marque.

In 1912 Packard introduced its first six-cylinder engine and a variety of new coachwork in more than a dozen different styles, with prices ranging from $5,000 to $6,550. The new Packard six was a 525-cubic-inch T-head design, with a bore and stroke of 4 1/2x5 1/2 inches and an output rated at 48 ALAM (Association of Licensed Automobile Manufacturers) horsepower. This was actually an inaccurate horsepower rating, and output from the T-head six was more on the order of 74 horsepower. Horsepower increased to 82 at 1,720 rpm on the 1913 models. Combined with the Packard Eighteen and Thirty, the new six-cylinder models brought more people to East Grand Boulevard's doorstep than ever before. The Packard Six, later to become known as the "48," was one of the fastest automobiles on the road, a favorite of both America's café society and the criminal world, which regarded the Packard Six as the fastest getaway car for the money. And indeed it was, capable of 0 to 60 in 30 seconds from a standing start and a top speed of 80 miles per hour.

In 1913, Packard added a second six-cylinder model, the "38," with a smaller displacement, more

reserved output, and a lower price, closing the books on the earlier Packard Model Eighteen.

Packard made a handsome profit in 1912 and the following year expanded its six-cylinder model lines and body offerings. By the close of the 1913 model year, Packard had produced a record 3,994 vehicles, making a profit of $2.2 million on $15.1 million in sales.

In 1914, Packard sixes were available in 20 different body styles and in both "38" and "48" series. Mechanical improvements to the driveline, engine, and suspension on all Packards made 1914 models the best riding and handling cars that had yet come from East Grand Boulevard. The new series 4-48 was powered by an L-head engine displacing 525 cubic inches, with a bore and stroke of 4 1/2x5 1/2 inches, and output of 82 horsepower. The 3-38 for 1914 featured a 415-cubic-inch L-head six with a bore and stroke of 4x5 1/2 inches, developing 65 horsepower. The cars were virtually carried over without any significant changes into 1915, and for good reason. Waiting in the wings was Packard's next and greatest achievement in the automotive industry—the Twin Six.

If building on the strengths of its prestige image was the goal, then 1915 was truly a watershed period for Packard. This was the year that East Grand Boulevard stunned the automotive industry with the introduction of the first 12-cylinder automobile put into series production anywhere in the world. Designed by Packard's new chief engineer, Jesse Vincent, who joined the firm in 1912, the Twin Six so improved production techniques that the cars sold for less than the previous six-cylinder models! With a base price starting at only $2,750 for the short 125-inch wheelbase five-passenger phaeton, Packard had not only built a more refined and more powerful car, but had built it for less.

The new V-12 engine was actually comprised of two banks of L-head cylinders vee'd at a narrow 60-degree angle. The Twin Six had a swept volume of 424 cubic inches with a bore and stroke of 3x5 inches and a near silent output of 85 horsepower at 3,000 rpm.

At the time of its introduction, on May 1, 1915, the Twin Six marked the greatest single advancement in automotive design since the debut of the Mercedes in 1901. Following Packard's return to

One of a handful of custom-bodied models produced on the 1916 Twin Six chassis, this example is a cloverleaf roadster. Note the enclosed rear seating area, rear quarter window curtain, carriage-like body motif, and unusual dual rear spares. A most unusual car for 1916. *National Automotive History Collection, Detroit Public Library*

Progressing toward the end of the decade, this Third Series (August 1917 to August 1919) Twin Six touring car was produced just prior to the factory ceasing automobile production in September 1918 to manufacture Liberty aircraft engines for World War I. *National Automotive History Collection, Detroit Public Library*

𝒫ackard was selected to provide the pace car in 1919, for the first post-World War I Memorial Day Classic. The car was a Twin Six roadster. The driver was none other than the car's chief designer, Jesse Vincent.

commercial automobile production, which had been suspended during World War I to manufacture Liberty aircraft engines, the Twin Six became one of the most prestigious automobiles sold in America. The stately 12-cylinder Packards were the cars of choice for film stars, industrialists, politicians, and heads of state. In 1921 President-elect Warren G. Harding road down Pennsylvania Avenue to the White House in a Twin Six, the first time an automobile was prominently featured in an inaugural parade.

The big Packard was the most successful car of its time, often referred to as "the Rolls-Royce of America." No other model in the company's history did more to solidly establish the Packard name than the Twin Six.

The Twin Six remained in production until 1923, the longest of any model up to that time, accounting for a staggering total of 35,000 cars, and elevating Packard to one of the world's leading manufacturers of luxury automobiles.

Packard resumed production of the Twin Six immediately after the Armistice, and this handsome 1919 Third Series Twin Six brougham, body-type 184, was among several stately closed coachwork designs offered that year. *National Automotive History Collection, Detroit Public Library*

$\mathcal{F}$our

$\mathcal{P}$ackard $\mathcal{S}$ets the $\mathcal{S}$tandard

THE AMERICAN LUXURY CAR FROM 1920 TO 1929

With the Twin Six as its flagship, Packard sailed into the 1920s with a stunning line of automobiles to rival any on either side of the Atlantic. From 1917 to 1918, Packard contributed to America's effort in World War I by producing 6,500 12-cylinder Liberty aircraft engines. Following the Armistice in November 1918, driving a Packard Twin Six was tantamount in the eyes of many to piloting an aircraft. Twelve had become Packard's lucky number.

The 1920s marked a well-defined shift from the previous two decades, when nearly half of the country's population lived in rural areas and on farms. Now more people were moving to the cities, and the cities were spreading block by block farther into what had once been considered the outskirts of town. Taller and larger buildings were erected, industry grew, and from Main Street to the Lincoln Highway, roads were built across the land. The automobile was fast becoming the most popular means of personal transportation.

Within Packard, change was also at hand. Henry Joy retired in 1916, and his general manager, Alvan Macauley, became president of the Packard Motor Car Company, a position he would hold until 1938. With

Twin Six sales booming along, Packard prepared a new, lower-priced companion model, the Single Six.

In the decade of the Roaring Twenties, the American automobile industry made some of its greatest advances, but for Packard the first two years were disappointing ones. The Single Six, introduced in the fall of 1920, was half the engine and half the prestige of the Twelve. To the surprise of Macauley and the board of directors, this was not well received by Packard customers. The cold shoulder turned toward the Single Six was no doubt compounded by a mild economic depression that occurred in 1920, and by year's end Packard found itself with nearly half of the Single Six models produced unsold and sitting in dealer inventory.

Sales of the smaller Packard limped along during 1921, while the Twin Six sold well, as did Packard trucks, one of the best commercial vehicles on the American market. After reviewing the shortcoming of the Single Six, Packard management determined that the problems were threefold: wheelbase length, styling, and the lack of a model that would accommodate more than five passengers. Thus, the 1922 model line was completely overhauled with all-new body styling, the choice of two wheelbases, 126-inch and 133-inch, and a seven-passenger model. Unfortunately, these

---

The 1920–21 Single Six was a scaled-down Twin Six. While handsomely proportioned, it was not well received by Packard customers as a low-priced leader. The five-passenger sedan was among the more luxurious interpretations on the 116-inch-wheelbase Single Six, which was also offered as a five-passenger touring, two-passenger roadster, and four-passenger coupe. *National Automotive History Collection, Detroit Public Library*

OPPOSITE

The Third Series Twin Six kicked off the 1920s for Packard as one of the most popular luxury cars in the country, ahead of Cadillac, Peerless, and Pierce-Arrow. The 1920–23 Packard 3-35 (often called Fourth Series) produced from August 1919 through June 1923 featured a 136-inch wheelbase and 90-horsepower 12-cylinder engine. The body style pictured was the popular five-passenger phaeton. *National Automotive History Collection, Detroit Public Library*

changes could not be completed until February, and approximately 1,384 of the older Model 116 Sixes were carried over into the 1922 model year before the new Model 126 and Model 133 Single Sixes were introduced.

It was the styling, as it turned out, more than anything else that really caught the public's eye. The first Single Six was a scaled-down version of the Twin Six, and it gave the impression of being less car. With sportier styling and a slight boost in performance, the new Single Six made Packard history generating some $10 million in retail sales during its first 40 days! By midyear, Packard dealers and distributors were clamoring for more Single Sixes than the company could possibly produce. The overcapacity that plagued Packard in 1920 and 1921 turned into a backlog of orders.

Throughout the early 1920s, Packard continued to increase its share of the luxury car market. In 1923 the men of East Grand Boulevard stunned the Detroit establishment by announcing that both the Twin Six and the entire line of Packard trucks were to be discontinued at the end of the model year. For 1924 there awaited a new model to take on the mantle of Packard's luxury leader, the Single Eight.

The innovative new Packard was the first volume-produced American automobile to offer both an inline eight-cylinder engine and four-wheel brakes. Previously, only the limited-production Model A Duesenberg had offered this level of mechanical sophistication, and in Europe one would have had to purchase the most expensive luxury makes, such as Isotta-Fraschini, to find comparable features.[1]

By 1925 the highly successful new model came to be known as the Packard Eight (consequently, the now junior six-cylinder line was renamed the Packard Six) and was available with an ever-increasing variety of factory and custom-built coachwork. The Packard Eight was offered in two wheelbase lengths, 136-inch and 143-inch, and in 12 cataloged factory bodies, along with what Packard advertised as "Original Creations by Master Designers" on the long wheelbase chassis. These were presented in a special custom catalog and included a four-passenger sedan cabriolet bodied by Judkins, a five-passenger stationary town cabriolet by Derham, a similarly styled town cabriolet model bodied by Fleetwood, a seven-passenger inside-drive limousine sedan built by Holbrook, and three

The stylish First Series 1922–23 Packard 126 touring was at the vanguard of the revised Single Six line. Built on a new, longer 126-inch wheelbase, and powered by a slightly more agile engine developing 54 horsepower, the touring, priced at only $2,480, was one of 11 new body styles introduced in 1922. *National Automotive History Collection, Detroit Public Library*

The Second Series 226 models were renamed Packard Six and, with styling that ranged from sporty to very elegant, such as this 1924 sedan, became one of East Grand Boulevard's best-selling cars. The Packard Six shared many aspects of the new Packard Eight's engineering, including four-wheel brakes, service-brake-activated stoplight, rearview mirror, and divided windshield. *National Automotive History Collection, Detroit Public Library*

*I*n the halcyon days before animal rights activists, many a great cat gave up its coat to the ladies of social prominence, and this combination of leopard and mink worn by actress Gilda Gray was certainly in vogue with the regal 1924 Packard Single Eight seven-passenger sedan. In the background is the Packard Motor Car Company building on East Grand Boulevard. *National Automotive History Collection, Detroit Public Library*

*S*ome young socialites preferred to have their fur on a leash, like this elegant Borzoi (more popularly known in the 1920s and 1930s as a Russian wolfhound). The car is a 1925 Model 243, seven-passenger sedan limousine built on the long 143-inch-wheelbase chassis. The 357.8-cubic-inch displacement Packard Eight beneath the long gracefully curved Packard hood delivered 85 horsepower at 3,000 rpm. *National Automotive History Collection, Detroit Public Library*

custom models designed by Dietrich, a five-passenger stationary town cabriolet, a two-passenger convertible coupe, and a four-passenger sedan.

Automotive stylist Raymond Dietrich was responsible for designing a significant number of what we consider today to be *classic* Packards. Dietrich had a way with the subtlety of a bodyline, its implications and dynamics, quite unlike any other stylist of the era. No one could do so little to a car's appearance yet make so great a difference. A slight variation in an angle, another crease added here, a

faint drop there, and miraculously a car had a distinctive look all its own. A "Custom Body by Dietrich" was more than an automobile; it was a signed piece of art. Packard President Alvan Macauley knew that long before he hired Ray Dietrich under contract as Packard's "Body Critic" in 1925.

"In Ray Dietrich," wrote historian C. A. Leslie Jr. in *Packard A History of the Motor Car and the Company*, "Macauley had found an amalgam of talents seldom assembled in a single individual. His background at the American Banknote Company eminently

Cataloged by Packard Motor Car Company on August 4, 1924, this photo was taken to promote the Second Series Six produced from December 27, 1923, through February 2, 1925. Packard's basic four-passenger coupe, the car was priced at $3,275. Coupes were built on the short 126-inch wheelbase. *National Automotive History Collection, Detroit Public Library*

One of the most elegant models in Packard's 1925–26 236 Second Series Eight line was the five-passenger touring car. Once again proving Packard's claim that "Better than one out of every five governors of the United States is a Packard owner," this car was owned by John G. Winant (pictured behind the wheel), the governor of New Hampshire. The car was fitted with the Packard DeLuxe emblem, twin side lamps attached to the windshield frame, and a folding rear tonneau windshield with wind wings. *National Automotive History Collection, Detroit Public Library*

Roaring Twenties film star Leatrice Joy behind the wheel of a 1926 Third Series Packard Six runabout. The photograph was taken for a publicity piece titled "Serving Susan," presumably about the attention ladies receive at Packard garages. The photo was taken at the Earle C. Anthony Packard Service Station and published in the summer 1926 issue of *The Packard* magazine. *National Automotive History Collection, Detroit Public Library*

qualified him as a line sketch artist, while his four years at Mechanics Institute had further developed his ability in drafting, illustrating, airbrush technique, surface development of body contours, and preparation of working drawings for detail parts and construction supervision. All this combined with 12 years practical experience, a natural creative ability, and a finely-honed knack for salesmanship." Ray Dietrich was a one-man design house.

Throughout the late 1920s and early 1930s, Dietrich penned designs that in many ways epitomize Packard's greatest era. From his visions of what an automobile should look like, Dietrich proposed features that would neither copy nor embellish on existing trends but rather establish new standards other auto makers would follow.

In the early 1920s, Ray Dietrich was one of the founding partners of LeBaron Carrossier in New York, along with associates Thomas Hibbard and Ralph Roberts. Hibbard later went on to join Howard "Dutch" Darrin, forming Hibbard and Darrin of Paris. Hibbard returned from France in the early 1930s and went to work for Harley Earl in the General Motors Art and Colour Section. Following Dietrich's departure in 1927, Roberts continued at the LeBaron helm with his multitalented assistant, sketch artist Roland Stickney. Thus from LeBaron had come four of the greatest automotive designers of the 1930s, Howard "Dutch" Darrin, Tom Hibbard, Ralph Roberts, and Ray Dietrich.

Dietrich left LeBaron to open his own design firm in partnership with the Murray Body Corporation of Detroit—then the largest supplier of sheet metal stampings in the auto industry. Unfortunately, Murray was in deep financial trouble. Despite its size, the company was losing money on almost every body it built, and in December 1925 was taken over by the Guardian Trust Company of Detroit, which had hired Frederick R. Robinson, a former Packard executive, to oversee Murray operations. The plan was to make Dietrich Inc. the custom body division of Murray. Dietrich, however, chose to distance himself from the parent company, moving into a separate building that put him near the Packard factory on East Grand Boulevard.

Interestingly enough, Dietrich's principal client in 1927 was Edsel Ford and the Lincoln Motor Company, which had helped fund the recapitalization of Murray; but Dietrich managed to work both sides of the street, in a manner of speaking. In addition to designing cars for Lincoln, he had the agreement with Macauley of Packard, and by the end of the year he was at work on a new series of semicustom designs that would be built exclusively for Packard.

Alvan Macauley was anxious to begin offering a line of "Custom Body by Packard" and "Body by Dietrich Inc." models, having reasoned, and rightly so, that more profit could be made by producing custom bodies in-house than by having an independent coachbuilder do the work on the outside. Of course, Murray-Dietrich Inc. would build the bodies for Packard. All very neat, but this did not eliminate the need for custom coachwork by LeBaron, Rollston, Holbrook, Judkins, and even Dietrich himself, work-

ing independently of Dietrich Inc. Macauley could now offer Packard customers an interesting new option—semicustom coachwork by Dietrich nearly as exclusive in design as his coachbuilt models, but at a lower price. In retrospect, it was a brilliant marketing strategy. And it worked.

By 1929, Ray Dietrich had revamped Packard styling completely, from the flagship Custom Eight to the new Standard Eight. The Dietrich semicustom line had a noticeably different appearance, from its longer 145 1/2-inch wheelbase and taller, wider radiator shell, to Dietrich's distinctive trademark single beltline—a wide molding at the top of the door panels, narrowing at the windshield post, and continuing forward along the length of the hood to the edge of the radiator shell. This was to become a styling trait

that would distinguish Packard coachwork throughout the early 1930s.

For Packard and the American automotive industry, the 1920s started slowly with a recession and then roared into a decade of growing prosperity that witnessed momentous economic growth: the continuing expansion of America's highway system—of which both Henry Joy and Alvan Macauley had been strong supporters through the Lincoln Highway Association—and increased sales and profits for Packard. In 1925 the company posted its greatest production, sales, and earnings year in history with a profit of more than $12 million. It was noted in *The Packard*, the company's official publication, that Packard automobiles were among the most popular in the country with politicians. "Better

*F*ilm stars loved Packards, so too did the people behind the stars, or in this instance, the people in charge of them. Pictured is Louis B. Mayer, Metro-Goldwyn-Mayer president, with his 1927 Packard Eight four-passenger coupe. Mayer's car was specially equipped with a horn mounted in front of the radiator, the DeLuxe radiator mascot, adjustable red lights mounted on the windshield pillars, and a step plate on the running board. The picture was taken on the MGM lot in Hollywood. *National Automotive History Collection, Detroit Public Library*

than one out of every five governors of the United States is a Packard owner," claimed the publication's editors, adding that "three Associate Justices and a former Associate Justice have cast a Packard ballot for their personal cars." So too had Chief Justice of the Supreme Court, William Howard Taft, Secretary of State Frank B. Kellogg, Speaker of the House Nicholas Longworth, and Secretary of the Navy Curtis D. Wilber. Packards were also the favored marque of U.S. diplomats, government officials in Washington, D.C., President Herbert Hoover, New York Governor Franklin D. Roosevelt, and of course, a majority of Hollywood celebrities who favored coachbuilt Packard roadsters, phaetons, and town cars over any other.

By 1925 the American automotive industry was riding on good times with nearly four million new cars sold that year and the birth of yet another new company headed by a retired General Motors vice president named Walter P. Chrysler.

*R*ay Dietrich produced a number of striking Individual Custom Eight bodies in the late 1920s. This is a 1928 Fourth Series convertible sedan with rear tonneau windshield. All Fourth Series Eights were built on a 143-inch wheelbase in 1928. Wire-spoke wheels were shown this year as production of the Packard Eight rose to 7,800 cars for the 1928 model year. *National Automotive History Collection, Detroit Public Library*

*A*nother handsome Dietrich Individual Custom Eight for 1928 is this rather reserved two-passenger coupe. Note the stylish dual rear-mounted spares and the use of a faux landau iron on the padded roof. Dietrich also added chrome trim around the windshield frame to further set off the gentle curve of the cowl. The Dietrich coupe had a rumble seat (indicated by the foot step atop the right rear fender) and a golf bag door in the rear quarter panel. *National Automotive History Collection, Detroit Public Library*

With increased sales and a substantial cash reserve in the mid-1920s, Packard improved its production lines at East Grand Boulevard and in so doing was again able to lower the retail price of the Packard Six based on new lower production costs and sales volume. Since it was first introduced in 1920, Packard decreased the price of the Six by more than half, making the car readily available to more people than any in Packard's history. The company also made optional color schemes available at no additional charge for the first time in 1927.

Packard increased its prestige image the following year by expanding the variety of custom-bodied models available from the leading American coachbuilders, all of whom had created stunning designs for the Packard Six and Packard Eight. Among 20 different Packard Customs in 1928 were models from Rollston, Holbrook, LeBaron, Judkins, Derham, Murphy, Fleetwood (just prior to its complete acquisition by GM), and, of course, Dietrich.

The 1929 Sixth Series models were built on two wheelbase lengths, 140 1/2-inch Custom Eight 640 and 145 1/2-inch DeLuxe Eight 645. Packard also had the lower-priced 319.2-cubic-inch, 90-horsepower Standard Eight on a 126 1/2-inch wheelbase and the very hot Packard Speedster, which used the short platform paired with the larger 105-horsepower 384.8-cubic-inch engine.

Sales figures were up again as East Grand Boulevard closed the books on the 1929 model year in August, noting that a considerable number of deliveries were under the heading "conquest sales," indicating that a customer had traded in a competitive make for a new Packard. As the company headed into the first model year of a new decade, it appeared as though the road to riches had no end in sight. But on October 28, 1929, America ran out of pavement.

Custom coachwork for Packard by Ralph Roberts and LeBaron Inc. was among the most impressive of any produced in the 1920s and 1930s. This 1929 Sixth Series Model 640 Individual Custom full-collapsible cabriolet was shown at the Cannes Concours d'Elegance and awarded the Grand Prize pennant and medal. The special LeBaron coachwork featured custom bumpers, a stanchion-mounted search lamp, a four-piece V-frame windshield, and dual step plates. National Automotive History Collection, Detroit Public Library

F *ive*

An American Classic

PACKARD MODELS FROM 1930 TO 1940

In April 1930, just six months after Wall Street was rocked to its foundation by more than a week of panic selling and newspaper scareheads claiming economic disaster, a seemingly optimistic Alvan Macauley stated that Packard would adhere "as closely as possible to a constant level of factory operations throughout the year, regardless of the irregularities in the market." Before the end of the year, however, sales figures were to tell a far different story. From model year 1929 to 1930, production declined from 47,855 to 28,386. By May 1930, Packard was in the midst of cutting its work week from six to five days and laying off some 2,000 employees.

Even with Ray Dietrich's outstanding new designs, Packard Eights were not doing well in the economic sea of despair that had washed across America. Neither, for that matter, were cars from the other auto makers. No one in Detroit really believed the Depression would last long. The general consensus was that the market would correct itself in a few months, and recovery would come in short order, as it had in 1920. Everyone soon realized, however, recovery was not around the corner. The Great Depression was.

Many companies, including Packard, misread the early signs, failed to look far enough down the road, or if they had, refused to accept what they saw, until they hit the wall. And what a bittersweet irony. During the height of this country's worst economic era, America's leading auto makers, Packard in particular, would produce the greatest cars in their history.

East Grand Boulevard's offerings, in addition to the Dietrich semicustoms, included new Dietrich Individual Customs, which would appear in the early 1930s with rakishly angled V-frame windshields—a design regarded by many as Dietrich's all-time masterpiece. This feature alone set the Packard Customs apart from all others. The traditional flat windshields that reigned throughout the remainder of the decade looked, well, *flat*, and very two-dimensional compared to the striking angles and chromed frameworks on Dietrich cars.

While his designs were dazzling, Ray Dietrich's tenure with Murray was something less, ending shortly after the Murray Body Company was reorganized as the Murray Corporation of America in 1929. With Murray under new management, Clayton Hill, a Packard engineer from 1911 to 1920, and the former assistant general manager of the Society of Automotive

---

*A*mong the many hood ornaments to grace the Packard radiator cap, the cormorant was the most popular. It's often called a pelican, and there has always been great debate over the actual name. A pelican was part of the Packard family crest, but as any bird watcher knows, pelicans have much longer bills and a far less graceful body. The bird depicted at the top of the Packard crest is most likely a cormorant and not a pelican. Introduced on the 1932 models, it was stylized throughout the 1930s, 1940s, and 1950s, remaining as the Packard symbol until the company's demise.

OPPOSTIE

*P*erhaps the greatest of Ray Dietrich's custom body designs for Packard, the 1933 Packard 1006 sport phaeton featured exquisite exterior styling, a rakishly angled V-frame windshield, and articulated ventipane fly windows that opened outward with the rear door. Only three Packard Twelve 1006 sport phaetons were produced in 1933. Dr. Joseph A. Murphy prides himself in owning two of them.

Engineers, was placed in charge of Murray, as well as Dietrich Inc., relegating the company's founder to a powerless figurehead. In September 1930, Ray Dietrich resigned.

In that same month, pending the announcement of the new Eighth Series models for 1931, Packard cut the prices on all remaining 1930 cars by $400 in an effort to generate more sales and attract buyers away from competitive makes to the lower-priced Standard Eights.

The sales that had been anticipated at the beginning of the year, however, failed to materialize, and by December 1930 Macauley's optimistic outlook turned to one of doubt about the future. On December 19, he wrote to the Packard Senior League: "Nobody knows how long this depression will continue, I have no way to predict definitely the course that our business, or business generally, will take from now on."

That course was to be a bumpy and difficult one, but Packard entered the 1930s prepared to deal with whatever the outcome, including the lowering of prices across the board midway through the 1931 model year (and a second reduction in

The 1933 Packard Twelve interior was a statement in elegance, particularly in the hands of Ray Dietrich. Packard instruments, surrounded with chromed bezels, had a jewel-like quality set off in tones of beige and black with black numerals. The instrument panel was all hand-finished burl wood, delicately edged with chrome trim.

Owner Ronald Benach of Lake Forest, Illinois, has traced the history of this one-off 1933 V-windshield Custom Dietrich coupe back to millionaire John Mecom. The car was purchased new by Mecom and remained in his family for some 25 years, until Houston, Texas, collector Charles Worthen purchased the car in the 1950s. Worthen kept the rare Packard Twelve for almost 40 years! Jerome Sauls of Warrington, Pennsylvania, acquired it for Benach in 1994, making him only the third owner.

A body by Dietrich, this DeLuxe Packard Eight Individual Custom featured reverse-hinged doors, chromed V radiator stone guard, twin trumpet horns, and the very stylish Woodlite headlights and parking lights. *National Automotive History Collection, Detroit Public Library*

price on remaining stock when the 1932 models were introduced).

The 1931 Packards went into production in August 1930 with the model lines designated 826 on the 127 1/2-inch wheelbase, 833 on the 134 1/2-inch wheelbase, and 840 and 845 on the 140 1/2- and 145 1/2-inch-wheelbase chassis. The 840 and 845 were consolidated into one line, with the longer wheelbase model being used only for the seven-passenger sedans and limousines. To further distinguish the Senior models, the Packard 840 and 845 came with the long sweeping front fenders that had been used the previous year on the 745 DeLuxe Eights. The "Custom" designation was also dropped, and all the large Eights were referred to as DeLuxe models. Pricing also reflected a change; the top models were more than $1,000 less than the previous year's 745 DeLuxe Eight and only $400 more than the 740 Customs.

Although mostly a carryover year, the distinguishing characteristics for the Eighth Series were larger hubcaps, steering wheels with three spokes rather than four, deeper fender lines, thicker running boards, and plain bumper clamps rather than paneled, as in 1930. Continued from the previous year was Packard's new four-speed transmission. Among a handful of new features, Eighth Series models were equipped with a vacuum-operated Bijur chassis lubrication system and a Stewart-Warner fuel pump, operated by a cam on the front of the timing chain

cover. Eighth Series Packards also received a considerable boost in performance with the Standard Eight developing 100 horsepower at 3,200 rpm, an increase of 10 horsepower from the previous year. The output on DeLuxe Eights was increased by 14 horsepower for an output of 120 at 3,200 rpm. Much of this added get-up-and-go came from the adaptation of the 1930 Model 734 Speedster's larger exhaust and inlet port design. The Standard and DeLuxe Eights used this same general type of intake manifold to achieve greater performance without having to increase the cubic inch displacement of the engine. The L-head straight eights had a bore and stroke of 3 3/16x5 inches on the Standard Eight, displacing 319 cubic inches, while the DeLuxe Eights displaced 384.4 cubic inches from a 3 1/2x5-inch bore and stroke.

The 1931 model year was highlighted by 23 body types: 1 for the Model 826, 11 for the 833, 9 for the 840 line, and 2 for the 845. The individual Customs had 9 body types each for the 833 and 840 chassis, 2 by Dietrich and 7 "Custom Made by Packard" styles. These represented the finalization of Packard's long-desired resolve to make the Individual Custom line an in-house operation.

Of the catalogued models for 1931, the least expensive to the most expensive ranged from $2,385 (lowered to $2,150 in June 1931) for the Model 826 sedan to $4,285 (later reduced to $3,600) for the Model 845 sedan-limousine. The most expensive Individual Custom was the all-weather town car landaulet priced at $6,075. Sadly, just 12,105 Standard Eights and 3,345 DeLuxe Eights were produced during the 1931 model year. The lower sales figures were further compounded by Packard's early launch of the Ninth Series models, which included the new Light Eight, and East Grand Boulevard's resurrection of the Twin Six on June 17, 1931.

For dealers whose inventories were still heavy with 1931 models, Packard provided a face-lifting kit to give the Eighth Series cars the same appearance as those of the Ninth. The kit included a special V radiator shell and headlight bar, outside horns, and the Ninth Series twin taillights and bumpers. In addition, prices on 1931 models still in stock were further reduced.

In 1932, Packard offered 10 body styles for the 903 DeLuxe Eight. The top model, priced at $4,550, was the stylish convertible sedan designed by Ray Dietrich and bodied for Packard by Murray. Part of the Individual Custom line in 1931, the Dietrich convertible sedan was added to the DeLuxe Eight Series in 1932, with the conspicuous absence of the distinguished Dietrich emblem

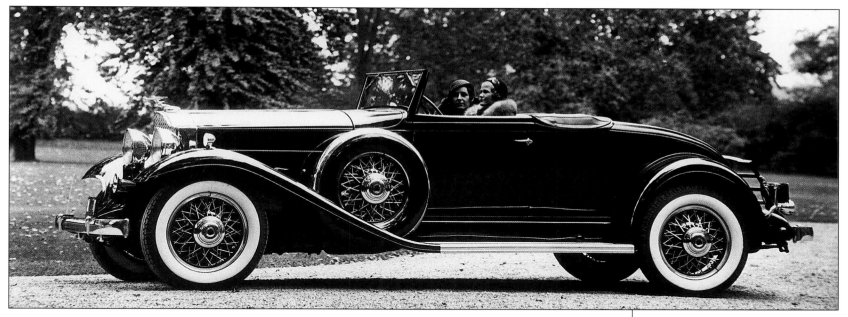

Among the best-styled models of the early 1930s was the Model 902 Packard Eight coupe-roadster. This fully equipped 1932 example features the DeLuxe radiator mascot, radiator stone guard, twin trumpet horns, dual side-mount spares, and chromium-plated wheels. *National Automotive History Collection, Detroit Public Library*

The sportiest Packard ever built was the 1934 LeBaron 1106 runabout speedster. The design was based on the Packard Model 734 speedster and Ed Macauley's Twin Six speedster (pictured with Macauley in 1933), originally done in 1932 and revised the following year with the extended pontoon fenders. The 1934 LeBaron 1106 speedsters were built in very limited numbers. Of the handful produced, one was ordered by Douglas Fairbanks and another by Carol Lombard as a gift to Clark Gable. The cars sold for $7,745, making them among the most expensive Packard models of the early 1930s. *Dave Holls collection*

on the body. The high-spirited Dietrich coachwork was also available on the new Packard Twin Six, built on the 142 1/8-inch wheelbase model 905 chassis.

The Ninth Series 903 was a blend of the old and the new for Packard. Old were the 19-inch wheels, large headlights, and unskirted fenders. Additionally, it marked a change from Packard's four-speed transmission to a new three-speed synchromesh with vacuum clutch, introduced by the end of the model year.

One of the most significant new features for 1932 went mostly unseen, except by coachbuilders. It was Packard's new double-drop X-braced frame, which provided more usable interior space and a lower overall body height without sacrificing headroom. The new Packards also came with a standard harmonic stabilizer front bumper, fender lamps, and dual trumpet horns. Yet even with all of these features at no additional cost, and very reasonable pricing overall, the new Senior Packard line failed to generate a profound increase in sales.

The Eleventh Series 1107 Packards, produced from August 1933 through August 1934, have come to be regarded as the finest models ever produced by Packard.

The Return of the Twin Six

While it may have appeared a bit ill-timed, in 1932 Packard dusted off the Twin Six name once again and introduced a brand new 12-cylinder engine, offered as an option on the DeLuxe Eight chassis. The Twin Six of 1932 was a byproduct of Packard's plans in 1930 to develop a 12-cylinder, front-wheel-drive automobile to compete with the new Cord. The engine, as well as the entire Packard front-wheel-drive concept, was the work of Cornelius Van Ranst. Before coming to Packard, Van Ranst worked with Leon Duray, Harry Miller, and Leo Goossen on the prototype Cord L-29. At the urging of Indianapolis 500 winner and Packard consultant Tommy Milton, the company hired Van Ranst in 1930. Although the front-wheel-drive model never materialized, the V-12 engine was just what Packard needed to keep pace with Cadillac.

With the new Twin Six, the men of East Grand Boulevard set their sights high, suggesting that the car would be a competitor, not to the 12-cylinder Lincolns or Cadillacs, but rather to the Marmon and Cadillac V-16s. This was a pretty aggressive goal, but as it turned out, reasonable enough, given the Packard's performance and price compared to the larger and more costly 16-cylinder Cadillac.

When the first Twin Six was delivered in April 1932, it boasted an output of 160 horsepower from a 445.5-cubic-inch displacement and was certified to reach 100 miles per hour. Twin Six models, and later Packard Twelves, were accompanied by a "Certificate of Approval" signed by two-time Indy 500 winner (1921 and 1923) Tommy Milton and Charlie Vincent, director of the Packard Proving Grounds, attesting that the car had been driven 250 miles and conformed, quoting Packard, "to the best Packard standards in acceleration and maximum speed, in control including steering, speed changes and brakes, in roadability and riding qualities, and in all adjustments necessary for . . . all riding and driving conditions."

The Twin Six was vested with a sumptuous variety of body styles, designed for Packard by Ray Dietrich. On two wheelbase lengths, Model 905 (142 1/8 inches) had 10 body styles available, and for the Model 906 (147 1/8 inches), 11 styles were offered, 9 of which were Individual Custom series.

The 1932 example pictured, owned by *Tonight Show* host Jay Leno, is a Model 905-style 578 coupe with rumble seat. It sold for $4,150 and was the lowest-priced Twin Six model offered. The most expensive was the Dietrich Custom series all-weather town car landaulet, priced at a hefty $7,950.

A stately, handsome car, the 578 coupe offered luxury appointments, broadcloth upholstery, and like all Twin Six models, a new instrument panel, featuring an engine-turned fascia plated chrome over nickel and covered with a protective clear lacquer coating. Instruments, elegant in their design, were black-faced with chromed pointers and a raised tan band carrying appropriate black numerals. The 4-inch clock, a Waltham eight-day hand-wound dual mainspring type, rested to the right of the panel, balanced by the 120-mile-per-hour speedometer on the left. The entire panel was set off by a new instrument board with dark walnut finish. Not exactly a high-volume car, only 304 Twin Six models were produced on the 142 1/8-inch wheelbase for 1932.

The Twin Six, technically, was a single-year production, succeeded in 1933 by the Packard Twelve, which also featured an improved chassis.

Nineteen thirty-three fell well short of expectations, but was nevertheless a remarkable year for custom coachwork, most of which had come from the drafting board of Ray Dietrich. Among the finest representatives of Packard coachwork were the 1006 customs, which, aside from having exquisite exterior styling, featured remarkably advanced interior designs for the period.

The sport phaetons were built on the long 147 1/2-inch wheelbase 1006 chassis usually reserved for limousines and custom bodies. (In general, phaetons built in 1933 were on the 142-inch 1005 chassis.) Although Dietrich fenders and hoods were unique from standard Packard fare, the most distinctive characteristic of the sport phaetons was the integrated design of the dual windshields, dashboard, and doors. Dietrich's layout for the sport phaeton called for a sweeping dashboard that wrapped around the driving compartment and curved into the doors. Today we call it a "cockpit design theme." In 1933, it was simply unheard of. The same design was repeated in the rear compartment with the rear windshield cowl wrapping around into the tops of the doors.

The sport phaetons had another Dietrich exclusive, articulated rear wind wings. Mounted to the rear windshield, they were also attached via a chromed arm to a narrow track in the door, allowing them to swing up and out of the way when the door was opened. More visual than practical, it was one of those great little gizmos that owners liked to talk about and show off.

True phaetons, the Dietrich cars did not have roll-up windows. To button up the car for foul weather, the rear windshield could be lowered behind the front seatback, and the wind wings detached from the door track, folded in, and stored away. Side curtains were then used front and rear to close the car to the elements.

Although only three Dietrich sport phaetons were built on the 1006 chassis in 1933, the body design was used the previous year by Packard. There were two 1932 Twin Six sport phaetons and three 1932 Super Eights. As far as can be determined, there were only three Packard Twelves in 1933. That doesn't mean that there weren't more, however.

Even though only three are known to exist, said Packard historian, collector, and restorer Bob Turnquist, there may have been as many as five. "Since they were for use at the major auto shows, it would have been almost impossible to transport the cars around the country quickly enough," said Turnquist, "and they often built more

cars than reported." As an example, Turnquist related an incident that happened at Harrah's Automobile Collection over 30 years ago. "I lift up the head of this LeBaron phaeton, of which I was told there were only three, and this one was body number five!"

Historically, the number three was the most common for show cars just the same. Why? According to Turnquist, "Three was the most economical for an auto maker when ordering a custom body, because the cost of the second and third was usually little more than the price of one."

The Dietrich sport phaeton was such a striking design that even though it was already a year old in 1933, Packard chose to use it on its stands at the New York, Chicago, Los Angeles, and San Francisco Auto Shows. The sport phaeton's V windshield and wraparound interior dash panel were also used in 1933 on a custom Dietrich sport coupe.

Dietrich also penned a stunning convertible victoria, convertible coupe, convertible sedan, and a stately formal sedan, which Packard drew upon to fill out the year's offerings on the Twelve's 147-inch-wheelbase chassis, along with two LeBaron Custom designs.

In 1933, anyone desiring a full custom body had to purchase the long-wheelbase Packard Twelve, as the comparable Model 904 Individual Custom Eight, available in 1932, was discontinued, lowering the company's automotive bill of fare to 3 lines instead of 4. At the top was the Packard Twelve, replacing the 1932 Twin Six, available in 11 body styles on the 1005 Series 142-inch-wheelbase chassis and 9 variations with Packard Custom coachwork on the 147-inch Series 1006 platform. In addi-

tion there were 8 Dietrich and LeBaron-bodied Individual Customs. One step down, the new Super Eight, replacing the old DeLuxe, had 2 wheelbase lengths, the Series 1003, measuring 135 inches between the wheels and offered only as a five-passenger sedan, and the Series 1004, built on a 142-inch-chassis in 13 body styles. The low-priced leader Packard Eight encompassed the former Light Eight and Standard Eight models with four 900 Series body styles carried over from 1932 and built on the 1001 Series 127 1/2-inch-wheelbase chassis, and 13 body styles on the larger 1002 Series 136-inch-wheelbase chassis.

The 1933 model year was the shortest in Packard history. Alvan Macauley had delayed the debut of Packard's Tenth Series until January, and then halted production eight months later to introduce the 1934 models. As it turned out, the delay had no adverse effect on Packard sales, which still came up short as the Depression deepened. Even those with the money to purchase a new Packard did not, some just being conservative, others waiting to see if the administration of President-elect Franklin Delano Roosevelt could change the economic tide that had swept wealth and prosperity from every corner of the country.

The Tenth Series, perhaps one of the finest in Packard's history, had been up against an adversary the company could not challenge—its own reputation for building cars that lasted! In 1933, Packard owners tested that reputation by holding on to their older models a year longer. Packard still delivered 4,800 cars and earned a modest profit of $506,433 on $19,230,000 in sales.

Built on a massive 142-inch-wheelbase chassis, the silver convertible coupe pictured in this chapter in front of the train depot in New Hope, Pennsylvania, was one of 11 semicustom body styles offered for the model year, all powered by Packard's 160-horsepower, 445-cubic-inch V-block 12-cylinder engine. On the average, a Packard Twelve could accelerate from 0 to 60 miles per hour in just 20.4 seconds, a respectable time for an automobile weighing well over 5,000 pounds.

Although the 1107 was about as handsome as a convertible could get, Packard held its own trump card with the stunning Model 1108 Dietrich convertible victoria, one of five Custom Dietrich models offered on the expansive 147-inch wheelbase Packard Twelve chassis. This was one of Dietrich's most exquisite designs, with an elegant elongated hood covering the entire cowl all the way to the base of the windshield. Priced at $6,080, only three Custom Dietrich convertible victorias were produced in 1934.

*P*ackard owners didn't have to wait for the National Automobile Show to see the most luxurious Packards on display. In 1933 the Packard dealership on Broadway and 61st Street in New York staged an "Open Car Show" from May 13 to 20. At center floor is a Model 1004 Super Eight convertible victoria. At center rear is a 1004 Super Eight phaeton. The model at the left rear of the showroom is a Super Eight convertible sedan. In the very foreground the New York dealer displayed a 1901 Packard. *National Automotive History Collection, Detroit Public Library*

*O*ne of 11 Dietrich-inspired body designs for Packard's semicustom line, the 1107 Packard Twelve convertible was one of the most attractive American cars of the 1930s. It was Dietrich's desire to design convertibles that looked as good with their tops up as down, and in most instances, better with the top up, because that was how most were ultimately driven. Packard offered 10 paint colors in 1934, including this striking shade of silver. This example is from the collection of Dr. Joseph A. Murphy.

Because of the body design, it was impossible to hinge the doors at the front, thus the massive Dietrich Custom featured rear-hinged, or as they have become popularly known, "suicide-style" doors.

The 1108 was the crowning jewel of Packard's 1934 12-cylinder model line. As designed and bodied by Dietrich Inc., the cars were all true coachbuilt customs. Nine different body styles were cataloged, including this style 4072, the Custom Dietrich convertible victoria. Priced at $6,080, only three examples were produced in 1934.

The 1108 was powered by Packard's 473-cubic-inch V-12 engine developing 160 horsepower. This was the second largest engine for cubic inch displacement built in the 1930s. The largest was the Marmon V-16 at nearly 500 cubic inches and delivering a chest-swelling 200 horsepower, second only to the mighty eight-cylinder Model J Duesenberg for output and sheer straight-line acceleration.

The high point of Packard styling in 1934 was a trio of Model 1108 designs consisting of a dual cowl sport phaeton, town car, and all-weather cabriolet, designed by the stylists at Briggs and built by LeBaron, which had been a subsidiary of the Briggs Manufacturing Company since 1927. Of the three, the sport phaeton is regarded as one of the most beautiful cars designed. Only four examples were originally built, although many more exist today, having been bodied in recent years on restored Packard Twelve chassis.

*T*he Packard Twelve was a beautifully sculptured engine with a pale green enamel finish. For the 1934 model year, Packard Twelves could be ordered with aluminum heads and a higher 6.8:1 compression ratio. Output from the 7.5-liter Twelve was 160 horsepower. The standard engine came with 6.0:1 compression and cast-iron heads.

*T*he 1934 Packard Twelve dual-cowl sport phaeton by LeBaron has been called the most beautifully designed automobile of the 1930s, and it is hard to argue the point. Only four examples were produced in this exact body style, and another five have been built over the last 15 years as rebodied cars on original Packard Twelve chassis. The 1108 models were built on the 147-inch-wheelbase chassis, measured 159 inches in overall length, and weighed in at 5,130 pounds.

Another stunning Dietrich design was the 1934 convertible sedan, which also featured the stylist's chromed V windshield. The Dietrich custom called for central-hinged doors—front suicide-style, rear conventional. The car also bore the de Sakhnoffsky-inspired long hood design. *Dave Holls collection*

Of the many components that go into the making of an automobile, coachwork has always been one of the principal considerations. The body beautiful, or at least the body unique.

In the early part of the twentieth century, every automobile body was custom built, and coachbuilders were, for the most part, independent of any individual automotive marque. A body by LeBaron, for example, could have been found on any number of different chassis, and the same was true for Fleetwood, one of America's earliest coachbuilders (before becoming part of General Motors in 1926). But as time progressed and the automobile became more of a commodity, the assembly line assumed the responsibility not only for chassis, engine, transmission, and suspension, but for the construction of bodies as well.

Most auto makers viewed the in-house construction of coachwork as an economic move, a means of controlling costs, but in many cases, it was also to improve quality control. The demands of mass production did not contribute to the coachbuilder's art. Prices either went up, or quality went down.

The financially disastrous events that concluded the 1920s, however, proved that Packard and a number of other manufacturers who followed similar paths were correct in lowering costs and bringing as many operations as possible within the corporate sphere. For Packard, the commitment in 1925 to ". . . build all of

our own bodies when, and as, arrangements can be made to that end," proved to be one of Alvan Macauley's best decisions. Throughout the late 1920s, Packard increased the size of its assembly operations, building more and more standard cars in-house. Still, it was the expensive custom bodies that brought Packard the most prestige, either at auto shows or on showroom floors, and by the mid-1930s custom coachwork was less for profit and more for image. Thus, many of Packard's most outstanding efforts in the area of custom body design were directed toward show cars, which introduced styling elements that would later be incorporated into semicustom and standard models.

One of the most interesting Packard experimental cars ever built was the 1106 Sport Coupe. On December 6, 1933, the Packard board approved the

The car pictured, fitted with motor number 901-601, causes some confusion as to which of the four known sport coupes was actually built first and shown at the New York Auto Show in 1934. It is possible that this was the first car built, and that it originally had the steel roof and fixed rear quarter windows. After being purchased, it is believed that the original owner took the car back to the Packard factory to have it updated with the 1935 grille, headlights, and dash. It is also possible that the padded roof was added at that time. Based on the engine number, this would appear to be the case, thus making the padded roof example the original 1934 show car and the first of the 1106 sport coupes built. *Dave Holls collection*

The Car of the Dome

*F*or Packard, the Dietrich signature on a coachbuilt body had become a symbol of quality sought by those of means. Ironic in a sense, since the man whose name meant so much to Packard's wealthiest clientele had been working for Chrysler Corporation as head of exterior design since 1931!

The designs used by Packard in the early 1930s were all done prior to Dietrich's departure to Walter P. Chrysler's side of town and were used to form the foundation of the most dramatically styled Packards in years, the most important of which became the centerpiece of the Chicago World's Fair Century of Progress Exposition.

Packard produced as many formal cars as Cadillac and Lincoln in the 1920s and 1930s. To show how important closed cars were to the Packard image, a Dietrich-designed limousine, known as a special sport sedan, was chosen by Packard to represent the company at the 1933 Century of Progress World's Fair in Chicago.

Built along the waterfront of Lake Michigan, the Chicago Exposition's architecture was a brilliant montage of color and form, the latest in art deco, moderne, and contemporary designs. It was there, under the giant dome of the Travel and Transportation Building, which rose a majestic 12 stories above the fairgrounds, that an art jury was asked to designate one automobile to represent the epitome of motor car transportation for 1933. They did not choose a sporty phaeton or speedster, they selected the elegant Dietrich Packard.

Later known as the "Car of the Dome," the 1933 Packard was Dietrich Style 3182, built on an 1107 chassis. Dietrich's design, actually penned in 1930, featured a low roofline, V windshield, and sweeping fenders, accentuated by stylist Alexis de Sakhnoffsky's famed "false hood," which gave the car the appearance of added length by eliminating the cowl and taking the hoodline all the way back to the windshield.

The Dietrich Packard was not only selected for its exterior styling, but for its interior design and appointments, described by Packard in 1933: "Aside from its unique lines, this Packard is of special interest because of the costliness of its interior furnishings. All body hardware is heavily gold-plated and so are the steering column and instruments. Wood paneling and trim are highly polished burled Carpathian elm. Built into the back of the front seat is a cabinet extending the full width of the car. The right side is occupied by a full-length dressing case with gold-plated fittings. At the left is a cellaret with a drop door which becomes a glass-covered table when lowered. Upholstery is especially selected beige broadcloth. The exterior finish is called Sun Glow Pearl, a new finish which is gold, brown, or pearl, depending upon how the light strikes it."

Built on the 147-inch-wheelbase chassis, the "Car of the Dome" was updated in August 1933 to reflect new fender, bumper, and cowl vent styling for the model year, which began three months after the Exposition opened. A Packard crew came in and made the changes overnight, so the next morning the car had all of the new styling cues.

In a historical sense, this was perhaps the most important car in Packard's history. At the time of the Chicago World's Fair, the automobile, as a concept and recognized mode of personal transportation, was only 47 years old, yet among all of the cars available in 1933—Duesenberg, Cadillac, Mercedes-Benz, Lincoln, Marmon, Hispano-Suiza, Pierce-Arrow, to name just a few—this Packard was the one chosen to represent the automobile in its grandest form.

All body hardware in the "Car of the Dome" was heavily gold-plated, as were the steering column and instruments. Wood paneling and trim were highly polished burled Carpathian elm. Built into the back of the front seat was a cabinet extending the full width of the car, which contained a dressing case with gold-plated fittings and a cellaret with a drop door that became a glass-covered table when lowered. Upholstery was specially selected beige broadcloth.

The 1933 Packard displayed at the Chicago World's Fair was a one-off sport sedan designed by Raymond Dietrich in 1930. Style number 3182, the "Car of the Dome" was built on a 147-inch 1933 Model 1107 Packard Twelve chassis. Dietrich's design featured a low roofline, V windshield, sweeping fenders, and a long nose accentuated by stylist Alexis de Sakhnoffsky's famed "false hood," which gave the car the appearance of added length by eliminating the cowl and taking the hoodline all the way back to the windshield.

Late in 1933, Packard began construction of an 1106 model designated as a sport coupe. The sleek, fastback styling was penned by LeBaron and forecasted styling trends that would last well into the 1940s. This is the third car built in the series and features a padded roof and blind rear quarters. The car was photographed at the estate of Jerry J. Moore, who at one time owned two of the three examples extant.

construction of three 1106 chassis, less fenders, radiators, running boards, hoods, and so on, to be used for a series of custom-built Sport Coupes being designed in Packard's engineering department.

The Sport Coupe is believed to have been requested by Edward Macauley, son of Packard President Alvan Macauley and the head of the new styling division established in 1932. All three cars were designed by LeBaron but were completed in the Packard Custom Body Shop.

Many Packard customs, such as the Sport Coupes, were built under the auspices of LeBaron-Detroit and were unsigned when delivered to the Packard plant. They were then affixed with the "Custom Made by Packard" plaque and doorsill plates, rather than LeBaron-Detroit emblems. The Sport Coupes, however, are considered LeBaron designs by most authorities.

Production costs for the custom models were rumored to have been $18,000 a piece, even though the selling price listed by Packard was only $10,000. The $8,000 difference was considered inexpensive advertising for Packard, and the East Grand Boulevard auto maker got its money's worth out of each of the cars. One Sport Coupe was shown at auto expositions throughout 1934, and another of the cars was displayed on the showroom floor of Queens Packard in New York City for almost a year before being sold. Many of the LeBaron-designed features from 1934 through 1939 were portents of future styling. Packard designs by LeBaron (Briggs) introduced a number of styling trends pioneered on the 1106 Sport Coupe, such as a severely raked V-style windshield with a chromed carrythrough into the roof, and the fastback roofline, a design that became rampant in the late 1930s and 1940s. Among the cars that clearly show an influence in styling forecasted by the 1934 Packard are the 1937 Lincoln Willoughby five-passenger coupe, 1938 Lincoln-Zephyr coupe-sedan, 1938 Chrysler Royal Six Series fastback, 1941 Buick Century Sedanette Model 66-S, 1941 Cadillac V-8 torpedo sedan coupe, and 1947 Pontiac fastback coupe. Of course, before too much credit goes to Macauley and Packard, it should be noted that Cadillac showed a similar V-16-style Aero-Dynamic Coupe at the 1933 Chicago Century of Progress Exposition. The car created quite a sensation at the General Motors Exhibit and was put into limited production with Fleetwood building 20 Aero-Dynamic Coupe bodies between 1934 and 1937, for the V-8, V-12, and 16-cylinder chassis. All things considered, the 1933 Cadillac more than likely influenced Edward Macauley and

the LeBaron design studio's development of the 1106 Sport Coupe in 1934.

Although only three cars were originally authorized, four are known to have been built, three of which survive today. Each was different in minor features and all four cars bore a special design number, style 783. The three Sport Coupes extant are serial number 1106-783-4, engine number 901-601; serial number 1106-783-17, engine number 902-170; and serial number 1106-783-15, engine number 902-380.

The first of the four cars produced had a steel roof and rear quarter windows that did not lower. This was the prototype model built for the 1934 New York Auto Show. The styling of this car was echoed in Germany at the 1934 Berlin Auto Show by a Mercedes-Benz 500K Autobahn Kurier, which shared a remarkably similar appearance.

The second Sport Coupe was virtually identical, with the exception of the rear quarter windows, which were fitted with a cranking mechanism. When originally sold, in June 1934, the car did not have this feature, and it is believed to have been added around 1938 or 1939 by Rudy Creuter of Rollson Inc. Creuter is recognized as the originator of this styling innovation, which he introduced in the late 1930s.

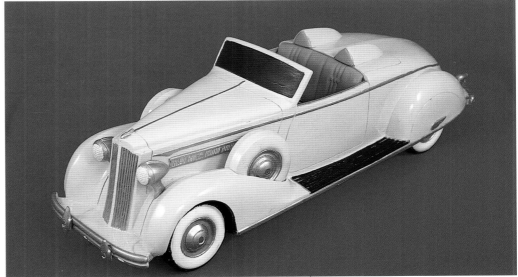

The padded roof model is considered the most stylish of the four examples built, although from a driver's perspective, the closed-in rear quarters produced the greatest "blind spot" ever conceived. The styling was nevertheless quite appealing.

The details of the fourth car are not known, but it is presumed to have been similar to the other three. There was also a possible fifth car built on the 1106 chassis, which was shipped to France in the late 1930s and lost during World War II.

Perhaps what is most significant about these cars, no matter how many were built, is the complexity of their design and the techniques and processes needed to produce them. The degree of hand labor that went into the Sport Coupe bodies, and the 1933 Cadillac which shared similar lines, contributed to further research into more efficient manufacturing techniques and more compliant materials.

In reviewing the manufacture of these cars, certain areas of construction presented great difficulty, mandating limited and costly hand-formed coachwork. The roof design of the Sport Coupe was highly complex, as were the trunk and fender designs, all of which required multiple pieces and extensive leading to complete. The pontoon fenders, for example, were hand hammer-formed over a hard maple styling buck and made in as many as four or five pieces. To hold the cars together, a stiff manganese bronze windshield frame was made—all time-consuming handwork. It wasn't until late in 1934 that the industry introduced the type of ductile steel that in a single pressing could completely form a one-piece turret top or fender.

All four Packard Sport Coupes were assembled on 135-inch wheelbase Super Eight chassis beefed up with altered rear springing. Packard Twelves were otherwise built on either the 142-inch wheelbase series 1107 chassis or the 147-inch wheelbase series 1108 chassis. The only other exception was the series 1106 275 boattail runabout.

Built to run at a sustained 105 miles per hour through special gearing, the axle setup on the Sport Coupes was from the Standard and Super Eight. The Super Eight chassis was chosen for its lighter weight and ability to absorb the greater torque produced by the Packard Twelve, and the shorter wheelbase also lent itself to the car's higher performance and sporty image.

There was one feature all four Sport Coupes shared, and for that matter nearly half of all Packard cars sold in 1934: a *radio*. Packard claimed the distinction in 1934 of being the first automobile manufacturer to engineer a radio into a car's design. To eliminate the problems that had, for the most part, made the automobile radio inefficient, shielded wiring and lead-in wires were used, the coils were changed to prevent static interference, and a specially designed instrument board was developed.

While the Sport Coupe design may have proved impractical in 1934, it made a significant contribution to later automobile styling. It is in such bold strokes of the designer's pen that we find the truly rare cars, those that are Classics in the truest sense.

The Eleventh Series Packards marked the end of an era in custom coachbuilding. At the height of the Great Depression, the demand for such elegant and costly models was on the wane, and even those who could still afford these extravagant automobiles were hesitant to flaunt their wealth in public. Thus, in 1935 Packard took a more conservative approach to design and marketing, placing more emphasis on the all-new lower-priced One Twenty and well-established Super Eight models. Love of the Packard Twelve, however, did not go unrequited.

To attract what buyers it could, Packard equipped the Twelfth Series models with an improved V-12 that developed up to 180 horsepower. The majority of cars sold were fitted with factory bodies, with only a handful being delivered with full custom coachwork, most of which went to America's aristocracy, government leaders, and film stars.

Packards were always popular among the Hollywood film colony, but there were a few actors who truly loved fine automobiles. Among them was Clark Gable, who it seems, when it came to cars, really did give a damn.

Gable owned dozens of expensive automobiles, from Duesenbergs to Packards, and mostly all with very sporty coachwork. To name a few, there was the famous SSJ Duesenberg, of which only two were built, the other for his friend Gary Cooper. Then there was Gable's custom-bodied JN Duesenberg. He was also seen at the wheel of one of Dutch Darrin's Packard victorias from time to time, and as legend has it, a 1936 Packard V-12 coupe-roadster.

One might wonder why Gable would purchase a production-bodied V-12 when there was a wealth of customs available in 1936. On the other hand, the coupe-roadster was one of the best-built production Packards of all time, so it may well have appealed to Gable just as it was.

Built on the Model 1407's 139 1/4-inch-wheel-base chassis, the coupe-roadster was one of 10 1407 body styles offered in 1936. It sold for just $3,850, the next to the least expensive model in the line.

The car was listed as body style 939 2/4 passenger. In simple terms, it was a rumble seat convertible with the first two of the 2/4—driver and passenger—comfortably seated within the leather-upholstered surrounds of the cockpit; the second couple, brave sporting souls that they would have to have been, got aired out in the open rear seat. A pretty basic premise for a four-passenger car, but on the Packard 1407 chassis it was downright sporty, and definitely Hollywood.

*W*hen the first Packard One Twenty, a four-door sedan, rolled off the East Grand Boulevard assembly line the first week of January 1935, Alvan Macauley (left) was presented the key to the city by Detroit Mayor Frank Couzens. *Department of Automotive History, Detroit Historical Museums*

*M*acauley and the management team went to incredible lengths to properly introduce the One Twenty not as the lowest-priced Packard ever, which it was, but rather as the newest and most innovative Packard ever produced. To show off the One Twenty, Packard's Jefferson Branch dealership in Detroit built the "Little Theatre" which showed patrons a short talking movie, titled *True to Tradition*, about the car's development and new design features. This was the most innovative and aggressive model launch ever undertaken by an American auto maker up to that time. *Department of Automotive History, Detroit Historical Museums*

Packard One Twenty models were rolling off the East Grand Boulevard assembly line in record numbers. Here a line of 1935 sedans are being readied for shipment to Buffalo, New York, and Cleveland, Ohio, via a Greater Detroit steamship. The cars were unloaded in Buffalo and driven to the dealerships. *Department of Automotive History, Detroit Historical Museums*

Packard had never been a mass producer and admittedly had no idea how to build a car in the quantities that would be required by the One Twenty. Packard began a search for someone with the manufacturing expertise to head up One Twenty assembly, and the company found George T. Christopher, a former GM man who had managed production at Oldsmobile, Pontiac, and Buick during his career. Known for cost-efficient production techniques, Christopher was hired by Packard as assistant vice president for manufacturing and production manager of the new One Twenty line. *Department of Automotive History, Detroit Historical Museums*

All Fourteenth Series Packard Twelves were provided the same styling changes as the Eight and Super Eight models in 1936, and in fact, the Twelve coupe-roadster body was almost identical to that of the Super Eight's.

Packard also offered the Twelve on a shorter 132 1/4-inch wheelbase Model 1406 chassis, but this one was available only as a five-passenger sedan. On the longer 144 1/4-inch Model 1408 chassis, Packard offered five factory variants. [1]

Factory coachwork for the Twelfth and Fourteenth Series models (bowing to superstition, there was no Thirteenth Series) provided the 1935 and 1936 models with a new, sportier profile through the use of a standardized pontoon-style front fender appearance, an adaptation of the Alexis de Sakhnoffsky–inspired false hood design. Carrying over a new headlight design introduced in 1935, featuring rounded rather than V headlamps and new, longer, bullet-shaped

housings accented with a chromed crest along the top, the Fourteenth Series Packard Twelve had revised front sheet metal to allow for a more pronounced slope to the radiator and grille shell.

Back in 1935, horsepower was raised from 160 to 175 (180 with high-compression heads) by increasing the stroke to 4.250 inches and displacement from 445.7 cubic inches to 473.31. This same formula was used again in 1936. For the model year, which ran from August 10, 1935, through September 2, 1936, a total of 682 Packard Twelve chassis were produced. Only a handful were coupe-roadsters, and of that, only one is known to have been equipped with a rear-mounted spare, the very model Gable was reported to have driven.

Nineteen thirty-six was also something of a benchmark year in a passing sense, the last in which Packard Twelves would come with a solid I-beam front axle and mechanical brakes. The new 1937 models would be equipped with Packard's "Safe-T-FleX" independent front wheel suspension and new hydraulic brakes.

"Less is More" might have been the slogan for Packard's Fifteenth Series. The Eight and Super Eight were combined into one model line with the new 1937 cars adopting the Eight's powerplant, now developing 135 horsepower, five horses better than the previous year, but 15 horsepower less than the deleted Super Eight engine had offered. The combining of Eight and Super Eight models also reduced the number of available Packard wheelbases. In 1936, the Eight was offered with 127-inch, 134-inch, and 139-inch lengths between the wheel openings; the Super Eight with 132-inch, 139-inch, and 144-inch spans. For 1937 the choices were limited only to those of the Packard Eight. For all intents and purposes, with the changes in engine and wheelbase, the Super Eight had effectively been deleted from the Packard line, replaced by an improved version of the Eight.

Packard formal cars for 1935 included the Super Eight Model 1205 seven-passenger sedan (left), built on the 144-inch wheelbase and equipped with the 150-horsepower engine; the Model 1201 Packard Eight five-passenger sedan (center) on the shorter 134-inch wheelbase with 130 horsepower engine; and Packard Twelve Model 1208 seven-passenger sedan with the 175-horsepower 12-cylinder engine and 144-inch-wheelbase chassis. Prices ranged from $3,390 for the Model 1205 to $2,585 for the Packard Eight and $4,285 for the Twelve. National Automotive History Collection, Detroit Public Library

At the very top of the Packard Twelve model line for 1935 was the custom-built Model 1208 all-weather town car designed and built by LeBaron and listing for $6,435. Body type L-194, the LeBaron design seated seven passengers. Both front and rear doors were reverse-hinged. The chauffeur's compartment could be sealed against foul weather by a fabric top. *National Automotive History Collection, Detroit Public Library*

The Packard One Twenty was the doorway to a new generation of automotive design and engineering for the men of East Grand Boulevard. The car's development in the early 1930s pioneered completely new technologies that would ultimately reshape Packard's Senior cars in the late 1930s. One of the aesthetic byproducts of the One Twenty was the handsome swept-back grille, pictured in this 1937 Packard publicity photo. *Department of Automotive History, Detroit Historical Museums*

Uncertain of what buyer reaction would be to the new consolidated eight-cylinder line, Packard made an unprecedented move, pricing the Fifteenth Series Super Eights some $50 *less* than the previous year's Packard Eights. And while the Fifteenth Series might first have appeared to be less of a car, Packard portrayed it to the public as an overall enhancement of the model line. More car for less money? In many ways the 1937 Super Eights actually were better auto-mobiles than their predecessors, and much of the credit was due to the design of the lower-priced Packard One Twenty introduced in 1935.

While the One Twenty had become the backbone of Packard's financial security in the mid- to late-1930s, it was the Senior line of Super Eights and Twelves that remained the standard bearer of the marque's luxury image, irrespective of the marginal profits such cars brought. The One Twenty, however, played a significant role in developing the 1937 Super Eight.

The Fifteenth Series was the first Senior car to benefit from technology developed for the One Twenty. The Super Eights now incorporated the medium-priced Packard's more advanced independent front suspension. The Super Eight also offered hydraulic brakes with centrifuge drums and two shoes for each wheel. Externally, a new, narrower, slanted radiator shell graced the Fifteenth Series' prow, as did new front and rear bumpers. Overall, the 1937 models were excellent cars. If not as large or powerful as their predecessors, they were as well built, as luxurious, and offered better handling and ride comfort, portents of an even more refined series of eight-cylinder Packards to come in the twilight years of the classic era, cars that would also evolve quite miraculously from Packard's lower-priced One Twenty models.

Of all the Senior Packards you're likely to see at a Concours d'Elegance, you'll seldom, if ever, come

The One Twenty very likely saved Packard in the depths of the Depression. The company posted substantial losses in 1931 and 1932, and only a very modest profit of $506,433 in 1933. The greatest loss, however, was to Packard stockholders. Shares had fallen from a pre-Crash high of 129 points to around 2 points by 1933. When the One Twenty made its debut, Packard suddenly was flooded with thousands of orders. For the first time the vast middle class could buy an eight-cylinder Packard, the car driven by presidents, kings, dictators, film stars, hoodlums, and captains of industry, for a starting price of just $850. The 1937 model pictured, a Fifteenth Series convertible sedan and the most expensive production One Twenty offered, sold for just $1,550. A comparable Ford model was $750. The highest-priced One Twenty was the DeLuxe seven-passenger limousine, which sold for $2,050. *Department of Automotive History, Detroit Historical Museums*

The Fifteenth Series One Twenty was offered for the first time with an eight-passenger station-wagon body. The cars were priced at around $1,595, and the wood-sided coachwork was also available on the reprised Packard Six chassis introduced in 1937 as a lower-priced companion to the One Twenty priced at $1,295. The example pictured, however, was a special one-off model designed by Brooks Stevens in 1937. This is arguably the best-looking station wagon ever built! *National Automotive History Collection, Detroit Public Library*

In 1936 the Packard One Twenty was chosen to set the starting pace for the Indianapolis 500. A convertible coupe driven by two-time Indy 500 winner Tommy Milton led the starting field for the 24th running of the Memorial Day Classic. The 1936 models had an output of 120 horsepower achieved by a 3/8-inch stroke increase and a new swept volume of 282 cubic inches. *Author's collection*

across a rumble seat coupe. Not that so few were ever built. To the contrary, the rumble seat coupe was a staple of the Packard model line from the late 1920s on through 1939, and because of this, the coupes were not that popular among latter-day collectors who preferred restoring Packard customs, open cars, and the more limited-production models. Based on the number of rumble seat coupes built by Packard over the years, you might expect quite a few to be around, but because the car was so common, only a handful were saved. Only six examples of the 1937 models are known to exist today. Rarity by attrition!

One of Packard's lowest-priced Senior models at $2,660, the 1937 rumble seat coupe was virtually identical to the business coupe, except, of course, for the folding deck-lid seatback. Built on the same 134-inch-wheelbase chassis as the Super Eight formal sedan, convertible victoria, and LeBaron cabriolet, there remained a considerable length of car both ahead of and behind the coupe's two-seat passenger compartment. Consequently, the interior was quite roomy, furnished with a pair of oversized seats upholstered in broadcloth.

Despite the trunk having been consumed by the rumble seat, the coupe still retained ample luggage space with a large, lockable storage compartment located just behind the front seats that was over a foot-and-a-half deep and the full width of the interior. In addition, the rear window could be cranked down so those enjoying the comfort of the front compartment could converse with their windblown passengers out back.

Close attention was paid to every detail of the interior appointments, from the sculptured art deco forms of the door handles and window cranks to the fine panel work of the instruments. Polished wood trim was used around the window frames and to accent the upholstered door panels, while the metal dashboard was painted with a wood-grained finish. It is by today's standards an elegant automobile, but no less than the average Packard owner would have expected in 1937, even from a standard coupe.

Among all of the great models produced during the 1930s, the 1937 Fifteenth Series Packard Twelve is considered to be one of the first really fine driving American cars, a car of both uncommon comfort and performance.

The Fifteenth Series Twelves, introduced in September 1936, featured new 16-inch wheels, Packard's "Safety Plus" bodies, made of hardwood and steel, and new "Double Trussed" frames, which factory literature claimed were more than 400 percent more rigid than

Built on the same 134-inch wheelbase as the Super Eight formal sedan, the Model 1501 rumble seat coupe left a rather lengthy rear deck behind the two-seat passenger compartment. With the high roofline, flat windshield, and painted radiator shell, the cars looked longer than they actually were, a clever subterfuge on the part of Packard's styling department.

before. The new models also boasted Packard's exclusive "Safe-T-FleX" independent front-wheel suspension and "Servo Sealed" four-wheel hydraulic brake system, features that had lofted Packard to the height of automotive technology in the late 1930s.

Powered by a 67-degree V-block 12-cylinder engine, the average 1507 model could accelerate from a stand to 60 miles per hour in under 15 seconds and attain a top speed of 85 miles per hour to 90 miles per hour.

To best use the Twelve's output of 175 horsepower (180 horsepower with the high-compression heads), Packard's three-speed selective synchromesh transmission was geared considerably low, providing quick throttle response and low-end torque. The Twelves reached their maximum power at around 3,500 rpm, with a standard final drive of 4.41:1. Packard offered both higher and lower overall ratios, ranging from 4.06:1 to 4.69:1 and 5.07:1. While the top end may have suffered some for the capability of reaching highway speeds in short order, the ride and handling in a Fifteenth Series Packard Twelve more than compensated for failing to reach that all-desired 100-mile-per-hour mark.

Packard sidemounts were always stylish, but by the late 1930s they had become an integral part of the fender treatment, adding to Packard's prestigious look.

The new independent front suspension instilled a feeling of comfort and stability previously unknown to Packard drivers. Additionally, the rear suspension now employed a Panhard rod, complementing the front suspension's antisway bar, and significantly reducing body lean. As such, the 1937 Packards were uncommonly agile for long-wheelbase cars, and at highway speeds handled far better than either the Lincoln or Cadillac Twelves.

The 1507 models, such as the Dietrich victoria, were built on a 139 1/4-inch wheelbase. The shorter-length 1506 was built on a 132 1/4-inch platform, while the long-wheelbase 1508 models measured 144 1/4 inches. The longest stretch available for the Super Eight model line was 139 inches, so if one wanted a really long wheelbase car, they had to opt for a Packard Twelve in 1937. This contributed to the Fifteenth Series being the best year ever for 12-cylinder cars, posting a record 1,300 sales.

Packard offered a total of 13 catalogued body styles, 1 for the 1506, 8 for 1507, and 4 for the 1508 chassis. The 1507 chassis could be bodied with factory coachwork ranging from the touring sedan, formal sedan, club sedan, coupe, convertible victoria, two- to four-passenger coupe, and coupe-roadster and to the custom-bodied LeBaron all-weather cabriolet.

As the decade of the 1930s neared its turbulent finale, the era of full custom coachwork had nearly come to an end, and almost all Packard bodies were being built in-house. Even the Dietrich-built customs were discontinued. All that remained was the styling and the Dietrich name, which would be dropped after 1937. The only true customs left in the Packard line were the LeBaron all-weather cabriolet and town car.

The soloist in Dietrich's swan song was the 1937 victoria, one of the best-looking cars in all of Packard history. Also one of the most practical. As an open car, it offered seating for four or five, and with only two doors, a far more sporting style with the same passenger seating as the larger and less graceful convertible sedan. The closest to the victoria in dashing good style was the coupe-roadster, which only allowed two to sit within the confines of the passenger compartment. Another couple could ride outboard in the rumble seat. The Dietrich victoria was the perfect compromise, the best of both worlds. From almost every aspect, inside or out, this was a handsome automobile, bold, yet at the same time elegant. An

accomplishment in styling that few cars of the era could match.

As the end of the decade approached, Packard designs began to take on a more contemporary look, and by 1938 when the sleek Model 1607 Sixteenth Series Packard Twelve was introduced, the styling of the trendsetting One Twenty and Packard Eight models had been integrated throughout the line. In fact, the Sixteenth Series Twelves were now built on the same chassis as the Eights and were offered with the same basic body styles. For the difference in price (better than double the cost of a Sixteenth Series Packard Eight), owners got a vastly more powerful engine and a superbly appointed interior.

The 1607 convertible coupe was one of the last great Packard body styles of the 1930s. The 1938 Packard Twelve was the ultimate driving car, with a massive 473.3-cubic-inch engine delivering 175 horsepower, an improved chassis and suspension design derived from the Packard Eight, hydraulic brakes with vacuum assist, and selective synchromesh three-speed transmission. The convertible coupe, or any of the one dozen body styles offered, represented the final evolution of the 12-cylinder models. These were discontinued in August 1939, marking the end of an era for Packard.

There was a time not so very long ago when formality was a matter of choice. A time when people dressed for dinner, even if they were dining at home. By 1940 many of those customs began to fall by the wayside. Times were changing, and in the automotive world those changes were about to send another long-established custom on down the road.

The New York Factory showroom always had the air of an auto show. In 1938 the display included a Packard Six chassis to highlight the addition of the Junior Series to the Packard line in 1937. *Department of Automotive History, Detroit Historical Museums*

OPPOSITE

*I*t was the end of an era for Packard and the American automotive industry. By the late 1930s, models like this 1938 Packard Twelve 1607 convertible were becoming more and more scarce, as was the individuality of the great multicylinder cars. For 1938, the 1607 and 1608 models were built on the same chassis as the lower-priced Packard Super Eight and shared similar coachwork. It was the mighty 175-horsepower engine that most distinguished these last great prewar Packards.

Throughout the 1930s, several large and well-established coachbuilders had been taken over by Detroit auto makers. Most, however, were forced to shutter their doors during the years of the Great Depression, and once-great names like the Walter M. Murphy Company were all long gone by the end of the decade. By 1940 the demand for custom coachwork had so greatly diminished that only a handful of independent coachbuilders remained in business. On the East Coast there was Derham in Rosemont, Pennsylvania, and in New York, Rollston was hanging on. Out west the top people from Murphy could be found working for Christian Bohman and Maurice Schwartz in Pasadena, California.

Bohman left Murphy in 1930, and Schwartz in 1932, when Walter Murphy closed the doors to his renowned shop. In April of 1932, Bohman and Schwartz formed their own company and hired most of the ex-Murphy staff. The scope of their business ranged from minor body modifications to complete frame-up designs, many for Hollywood celebrities and for use in movies; one example was the wildly styled Buick featured in the 1936 film *Topper*.

Packard began the 1940s with a stellar line of cars introduced in October 1939 at the 40th National Automobile Show in New York. The 1940 model line was one of Packard's most extensive, and culminated the company's four-year marketing plan to offer a full range of competitively priced cars. There were two Junior lines, consisting of the low- to middle-priced six-cylinder One Ten, beginning at just $867, and the medium-priced eight-cylinder One Twenty, starting at only $1,038. At the upper end of the scale, Packard offered the new Super Eight One Sixty and One Eighty models, ranging in price from $1,524 for a One Sixty business coupe to a high of $6,300 for a Darrin-bodied One Eighty convertible sedan.

It is interesting to note that the average price of a Packard had come down to less than half of what it was in the early 1900s, and the lowest-priced Packard was now less than $200 apart from a Ford DeLuxe Eight.

Mechanically, the Packard One Sixty and One Eighty shared the same chassis design, four-wheel hydraulic brakes, selective synchromesh three-speed transmission, and 160-horsepower straight eight. With

NEW 1939 PACKARDS
World's Gentlest Riding Cars

TIRES

a bore and stroke of 3 1/2x4 5/8 inches, displacement was now 356 cubic inches. The new 160-horsepower engines were the first from Packard to use hydraulic valve lifters. (The lower-priced eight used in the One Twenty line displaced 320 cubic inches and delivered a conservative output of 130 horsepower.)

To distinguish the One Sixty and One Eighty models, the Senior cars featured more luxurious interior appointments, a different design for the hood louver grilles, enameled hubcap emblems, and the traditional Packard cormorant radiator mascot. The One Sixty models bore a new 1940s rendition of Packard's Goddess of Speed.

With the 12-cylinder line discontinued, the Custom Super Eight One Eighty took on the mantle of Packard's top model, offering 10 body styles in three series and wheelbase lengths: the 127-inch 1806, 137-inch 1807, and 148-inch 1808. The cataloged body styles included a standard club sedan, convertible victoria, sport sedan, convertible sedan (the latter three with coachwork designed by Dutch Darrin), a five-passenger touring sedan, formal sedan, touring limousine, eight-passenger touring sedan, and all-weather cabriolet and town car models with coachwork by Rollston.

The true *custom* body styles in the 1940 series were those cars bodied by Rollston. The Darrin-bodied cars, actually built by Packard, were considered semicustoms. In overall styling, the 1940 models were not too far removed from those of 1938, though somewhat refined for the Eighteenth Series with a narrower grille shell, extended forward by 5 inches and painted to match the body color, thus giving the hood the illusion of being longer. Stylish catwalk fender grilles were also added in 1940 to give the cars a fresh look.

Among a handful of innovations associated with the 1940 Packards was the introduction of sealed-beam headlamps and fender-mounted parking lamps with attractive, frosted white bullet-shaped lenses. Of all the new features for 1940, the most significant was the availability of factory-installed air conditioning, still considered revolutionary in the automotive industry. "Cooled by Mechanical Refrigeration in Summer" was the tag line in a 1940 Packard sales brochure. The new models were the first production automobiles to offer air conditioning. The factory-installed

Business was booming in 1939, especially if one believed this staged and retouched publicity photo taken outside the East Grand Boulevard factory marshaling area. Pictured are assorted 1939 Sixes and One Twenties. The car being loaded onto the haulaway in the foreground is a Seventeenth Series Model 1701 One Twenty touring sedan. *National Automotive History Collection, Detroit Public Library*

Hollywood Packard dealers never missed a photo opportunity. Here a 1939 dealer car is being provided for actress Dorothy Lamour. Department of Automotive History, Detroit Historical Museums

Sharing the same body styles as the Packard Six for 1939, the eight-cylinder, 120-horsepower One Twenty models were built on a new 127-inch chassis. The wheelbase change came the previous year when the One Twenty became the Seventeenth Series Packard Eight. This was only for one year, and in 1939 the One Twenty name was back. The model pictured is a 1701 2/4-passenger convertible coupe. The new model was priced at $1,288. National Automotive History Collection, Detroit Public Library

Weather-Conditioner, as it was originally called by Packard, was actually contracted out to Bishop and Babcock in Cleveland, Ohio, which equipped approximately 2,000 Packards with the rather bulky cooling system. It was discontinued after 1941.

The worst change Packard made to the 1940 line was the introduction of a plastic instrument panel. While the synthetic material looked elegant when new, the dashboards soon began to discolor and warp from exposure to sunlight and heat, and in time most of the instrument panels began to dry out and crack.

The 1940 Packard line was broad enough in pricing and model selection to suit just about any taste or budget without having to secure the services of a custom coachbuilder. For the discerning few who still desired bespoke (custom) coachwork, the handful of independent design houses remaining produced some exceptional cars. Among the finest was a one-off touring sedan designed by Bohman and Schwartz on the 148-inch 1808 chassis. Costing approximately $7,500, the luxurious long-wheelbase sedan was appointed with Honduras mahogany cabinets and door trim, pleated upholstery with matching door panel trim, and Persian lamb's wool carpeting.

Christian Bohman and Maurice Schwartz also made a name for themselves designing cars for the handicapped, and among several of the innovations they had patented was a retractable step to assist entry and exit from the rear passenger compartment. Upon opening the door, a step slid out from under the body. This feature was incorporated into the 1940 custom touring sedan, along with padded footrests, pull-down privacy shades, ash receptacles and cigar lighters built into the rear armrests, and a rear air conditioning duct located on the package shelf just behind the seatback.

The Packard body, as modified by Bohman and Schwartz, featured opposed door hinges (suicide front doors), a rakish windshield design, and the conspicuous absence of traditional side-mount spares and running boards.

Among a handful of coachbuilt cars produced in the early 1940s, the Bohman and Schwartz touring sedan was one of the brightest that shown before the light flickered out on the classic era.

One of the great coachbuilt Packards of the late prewar era, this 1940 Custom touring sedan was bodied by Bohman and Schwartz of Pasadena, California. The body featured opposed door hinges (suicide front doors), a rakish windshield design, pontoon-style fenders, and the conspicuous absence of side-mount spares and running boards. The interior was entirely custom-designed by Bohman and Schwartz.

Six

The Darrin Packards

A TOUCH OF DUTCH

In 1987, at the age of 80, coachbuilder Rudy Stoessel could still recall his friendship with Howard "Dutch" Darrin, as clearly as though they had worked together just the night before in the old Darrin of Paris shop on Hollywood's famous Sunset Strip. Stoessel built custom-bodied Packards to Darrin's verbal specifications. "The man didn't draw, but he certainly knew what he liked," recalled Stoessel. "He would say, 'Rudy, I want something that looks like this,' then he would describe it and I would make it."

Whatever artistic skills Darrin lacked, he more than compensated for it with an ability to explain every nuance of a design to a draftsman until it appeared on paper exactly as he envisioned it. He had been designing automobiles this way since 1922 when he returned to France and opened Hibbard and Darrin Carrossier in Paris with friend and fellow designer Tom Hibbard, one of the original founding partners of LeBaron.

Darrin's first independent designs had been completed a year earlier on a pair of Delage chassis Dutch purchased from Walter P. Chrysler in

1921. He designed his own custom bodies for the cars and sold one of them to screen star Al Jolson.

Darrin and Hibbard worked together in France as both designers and distributors, having also secured the Minerva franchise for Paris. Over the next nine years, these two Americans in Paris created some remarkable body styles and did much to advance the coachbuilder's art with their patented all-aluminum body framework known as *Sylentlyte*.

After the stock market crash in 1929, business began to fall off. Late in 1931 Hibbard was approached by a representative from General Motors, asking if he would be interested in returning to the United States to take a position with GM's new Art and Colour Section. "I replied that I was," wrote Hibbard many years later, "providing that the offer was attractive enough." GM offered to pay Hibbard $20,000 a year for two years and pay all of his moving expenses from Paris to Detroit. It was a good enough offer, and in March 1932 Hibbard returned stateside with his family. Darrin decided to remain in Paris and formed a new partnership with a wealthy banker named Fernandez. For the next five years, Fernandez and Darrin designed and built some of the most acclaimed coachwork of the 1930s.

"*The* very early cars," said Darrin shop foreman Rudy Stoessel, "were not like the later ones we did on the Sunset Strip. The first two still had running boards. We built one for Clark Gable and another for Chester Morris," better known as fictional film detective Boston Blackie. "The first two also lacked the cast-aluminum cowl and were fitted with handmade wood-frame cowls," said Stoessel. The construction of the first Hollywood Darrins was pretty makeshift. Clark Gable once said of Dick Powell's car that it "looks better the farther you get away from it." *Dave Holls collection*

OPPOSITE

A true Hollywood Darrin, this car was built in 1939, one of a dozen One Twenty victorias produced at the Sunset Strip shop by Rudy Stoessel and his staff. Serial number DR 121235CAL, the car was built for the Packard dealership in Pasadena, California, and sold to film star Preston Foster in 1940. After Darrin closed down the Sunset Strip operation in July 1939, Stoessel, his partner Burton K. Chalmers, and former Darrin employees Paul Erdos and Charles Rotzenberger, opened Coachcraft Ltd. on Melrose Avenue in Hollywood. Foster brought the car back to Stoessel in 1941 and had it updated with a Super Eight front end and side grilles, a new radiator shell, hood, and headlights.

As an independent designer, Howard "Dutch" Darrin (left), pictured in 1937 with his first Packard victoria, had more influence on the automotive industry than anyone outside of General Motors' legendary design chief, Harley Earl. It wasn't the number of cars Darrin built that made him influential, but the people for whom they were built. Recalled Darrin's partner Rudy Stoessel, "The Hollywood Darrins were real celebrity cars. Clark Gable, Tyrone Power, Errol Flynn, Chester Morris, Al Jolson, Ruby Keeler, Preston Foster, and Gene Krupa all owned Darrins." This first example was sold to actor Dick Powell. *Dave Holls collection*

Although an American, Darrin had spent most of his life in France and was something of a celebrity over there, having flown with the Lafayette Escadrille during World War I and becoming an accomplished polo player in the late 1920s.

Profoundly talented, Dutch Darrin was a flamboyant man often given to exaggeration, which also made him one heck of a salesman. With his thick Bavarian accent restrained by long, reflective pauses, Stoessel poked his finger at a picture of Darrin taken in 1938, remarking that Darrin was ". . . what you would call a playboy. He was as much a celebrity as the people he sold the cars to, although I think Dutch gave away almost as many as he sold!"

When Darrin finally returned to the United States, it was at the beckoning of film producer Darryl Zanuck, who had become friends with Darrin after meeting him at a polo match in Paris. Dave Holls, retired General Motors director of design, said Darrin was also friends with actors Errol Flynn,

Chester Morris, and Clark Gable. "I think they helped convince him that remaining in France was not a good idea and that he could do better building custom-bodied cars in the United States."

Darrin came to California to visit Zanuck in 1936 and later admitted that ". . . the handwriting was on the wall in the custom body business by then. . . . In fact it had just about knocked down the wall." He wrapped up his affairs in Paris the following year and returned to southern California, where he finally set up a coachbuilding facility in an old bottle factory located at 8860 Sunset Boulevard. For a brief period before the Sunset Strip operation opened, Darrin worked out of Crown Coach in Los Angeles, where he started his first custom Packard and a Rolls-Royce Phantom III town car, the latter for Countess Dorothy di Frasso. Both were completed at Darrin of Paris, under the skilled hands of Stoessel and Paul Erdos.

"He had big ideas," Stoessel sighed, "Dutch wanted to have the best people working in the shop, and for a brief time, he did." By 1938, some of the most experienced coachbuilders in the country were looking for work and Darrin found them. "We hired Paul Erdos, who had been with the Walter M. Murphy Company in Pasadena; Charles Rotzenberger from Crown Coach in Los Angeles; Harry Fels, who had worked for Auburn, Cord, Duesenberg; Joe Mechelli and Carl Korn, also from Murphy; and Oscar Haskey, a former Auburn-Fuller Inc. metal-worker. We were Darrin of Paris."

While Darrin honed his design skills with Hibbard in the 1920s, Stoessel worked in Buffalo, New York, as a coachbuilder for one of America's preeminent auto makers, Pierce-Arrow. He moved to California in 1929, "to get away from the horrible weather." Stoessel worked for several different coachbuilding establishments in the 1930s, until he hooked up with Darrin in 1937.

Dutch always had a fondness for Packards and was quick to acknowledge that Packard was the best car built in America. "Its chassis was unimpeachable—and its classic grille was a great starting point," he once said. Of course, Darrin subtly changed just about everything else on the cars from the grille back, selling the first example of what would come to be known as a "Hollywood Darrin" to film star Dick Powell in 1938.

Recalled Stoessel, "The Hollywood Darrins were real celebrity cars. Clark Gable, Tyrone Power, Errol Flynn, Chester Morris, Al Jolson, Ruby Keeler, Preston Foster, and Gene Krupa all purchased cars from us." Darrin Packards were almost synonymous with the Hollywood film colony, much to Darrin's own conniving.

Equal parts promoter, designer, and showman, tales of Darrin's attention-grabbing stunts became legendary in the industry, including one recounted by his friend and fellow stylist Alex Tremulis, who told a tale about Darrin dropping his pants in front of Henry J. and Edgar Kaiser to get their attention while they were reviewing proposals for the 1951 Kaiser. "When Dutch saw them heading toward another designer's work instead of his, he quickly unbuckled his belt, called out a greeting to Henry, and as he stepped forward to shake hands, his pants fell down around his ankles. Everyone broke up laughing as Kaiser walked over to Dutch, who reeled him in." Darrin got the job, which ultimately led to a long relationship with

Every Hollywood and Packard-built Darrin bore the distinctive signature script on the front or rear of the car . . . as if the cut-down doors and distinctive 3-inch-longer hood weren't enough of a clue!

Darrin did little to the Packard interiors, but what he changed led the way to one of the most important safety features of the post-World War II era. He padded the dashboard and wrapped it around into the tops of the doors. The instrument panel was now not only better-looking, but a bit more forgiving should one find their head in sudden contact.

A rare styling studio clay (about 2 feet long) done by Darrin in 1939 for a proposed dual-cowl phaeton. Although the car was never built, the basic lines of the model were used for the limited-production 1940 Darrin convertible sedan. *Model from the collection of Robert Turnquist. Photo by Dennis Adler*

the wheel of a Darrin Packard. By the late 1930s, he had become the toast of Hollywood and the bane of Detroit. At movie premiers, Darrin models arrived in front of the cameras more often. Once, he even had actress Ann Sheridan delay her exit from a film premier so that her car had to be brought around several times!

The Darrins were considerably different from the more refined and contemporary coachwork offered by the Packard factory. Almost totally redesigned, or so it appeared, Darrin Packards actually used as many original factory parts as possible. Recalled Stoessel, "Like Darrin, the cars were imagery."

The process of converting the Packard One Twenty into a Hollywood Darrin was nevertheless a project requiring considerable talent and skill. "Dutch started with the least expensive models he could buy, the Packard One Twenty business coupe. A real plain Jane, a Sally Rand of a car, a stripper," joked Stoessel. "He would buy them down in Texas for around $1,400 each from a dealer he knew."

To convert coupes into Darrin convertible victorias, Stoessel and his six-man crew cut the tops off the cars and fitted them with new windshields, a three-piece cast-aluminum cowl, and custom-made doors.

Henry J. Kaiser and the creation of one of America's first sports cars, the 1954 Kaiser-Darrin.

Back in 1937, Dutch was no less resourceful in guaranteeing that his cars, and their famous owners, appeared in movie newsreels as frequently as possible, often personally ensuring that a camera crew would be in just the right place at the right time to capture a celebrity behind

*T*he most expensive of the 1940 Darrins, the convertible sedan was built on the 138-inch-wheelbase Packard Custom Super Eight One Eighty chassis and sold for $6,300. Approximately 10 were built.

One of two Darrin-like sedans built by Packard in 1940 for the 1941 model year. Cataloged as a Darrin sport sedan, the body style was Type 1422 (the Darrin victoria was listed as Type 1429). The cars lacked the proportional balance of the Darrin prototype because the factory built them with off-the-shelf parts and left on the side mounts and running boards, the absence of which contributed to the Darrin's superior styling. *Dave Holls collection*

In 1940, Darrin produced a single custom-built sedan as an alternative design to the victoria and convertible sedan. It has often been thought of as Dutch's retort to Bill Mitchell's swank 1938 Cadillac Sixty Special. The Darrin, however, is probably just a little sweeter-looking. Packard produced at least two others, but they were not as gracefully styled as Darrin's four-door, with its long stretch of hood and an ever-so-subtle drop in the door line. *Dave Holls collection*

The running boards were removed and a 4-inch sill was added below the doors to strengthen the body.

Some of the styling changes made by Darrin were simple yet quite effective. For example, the rear fenders were removed, slightly stretched, and then rehung with a forward slant, while the front fenders were restyled and skirted to fit a body absent of running boards. The radiator shell was cut down by 3 inches, and the hood was sectioned. To strengthen the body after the top was cut away, a new rear deck panel and hardwood framework was fabricated for the rear seat compartment. The Darrin shop also produced the convertible top mechanisms, a complicated affair that Stoessel agreed was better left down once lowered!

Rudy Stoessel's own three-piece aluminum cowl, with left, right, and center sections, butted up to the hood, which was lengthened to give the Darrin cars their long, sleek appearance. The cowl was designed to cure the flex problems Stoessel had had

*R*udy Stoessel (center) and one of his assistants rework a Packard One Twenty chassis into a Darrin victoria at the Sunset Strip factory in 1938. The bodies were fitted with new windshields, a three-piece cast-aluminum cowl designed by Stoessel, and custom-made doors (note the new aluminum door frame behind the fender). The running boards were removed and a 4-inch sill was added below the doors to strengthen the body. Once production got underway on the Sunset Strip, there were usually six cars being built at any given time.

*T*he Darrin signature on this 1940 model appears at the rear of the car. Note the 1940 instruments and steering wheel and padded dashboard panel.

86

This 1940 Packard Super Eight Darrin convertible victoria is pictured with a Luscomb airplane, an equally adventurous means of transportation and quite a suitable companion for the Darrin Packard. Approximately 50 victorias were built by Packard as semicustom models. *Dave Holls collection*

Shown with the top raised is an Eighteenth Series One Eighty Super Eight Darrin victoria. The 1940 cars were built on a 127-inch-wheelbase chassis and were powered by Packard's 160-horsepower straight eight. This is an early example, as indicated by the early hubcaps. The car has the DeLuxe Packard hood ornament and optional white sidewall tires. *National Automotive History Collection, Detroit Pubic Library*

1942 Packard One-Eighty Darrin Victoria: An Owner's Tale

By Bob Turnquist with Dennis Adler

This is better than the old-car-in-the-barn story. This is the old-car-in-the-barn and the-original-owner-still-in-the-house story. Much better.

Rarely, if ever, does one find a car nearly a half-century old still in the possession of the first owner. Packard collector, restorer, and author Bob Turnquist did just that.

The story of Bob's 1942 Packard Darrin came to light when I visited him at Hibernia Auto in New Jersey to photograph his Darrin Packard. In casual conversation he mentioned that the Darrin was originally owned by a woman who lived just a half mile away. You can imagine my surprise when Bob said she was still alive. "She was 81 when I bought the car from her in 1981," said Turnquist. We decided that there could be no better place to photograph the victoria than at the home where this grand old Packard had resided for most of its life.

When we arrived at Mildred McEwan's home, the caretaker said to Bob, "I remember you, you bought the Darrin." It seems that the caretaker had started working for the McEwans along with his father in the early 1940s, and he remembered the times Bob Turnquist had come by to see the car. Mrs. McEwan was still living in her home at age 94; however, she was now bedridden.

"Mildred and Richard McEwan were married in their early 20s and had purchased their 28-acre farm known as *Blue Gate* in 1928. They were very nice people, and Mrs. McEwan is the only link I have to my past in the neighborhood," said Turnquist, holding on to the ephemeral image of his youth and the old wooden garage where he first saw the Packard so many years before.

"Richard McEwan had six brothers, and they owned the McEwan Mills in Whippany, New Jersey. In their heyday, they employed half the people in Whippany. In addition, Mr. McEwan owned a box factory in Newark, New Jersey, was the sole owner of the Morristown Erie RR, and CEO of the Board of the Whippany Bank.

"His wife finished high school and then took up the gentle pursuit of painting china, playing the piano, horseback riding, and social teas. I once asked her why she didn't go to college. She said, 'Young ladies of my era were not sent to college.'

"My first meeting with Mr. and Mrs. McEwan was in 1940. My parents had purchased a 40-acre farm a half mile away. Both farms were being raided by wild dogs that year, and they were killing our sheep. That was the catalyst that brought the Turnquists and McEwans together," recalled Bob.

Being a Packard lover since he was a youth in the 1930s, the thing that impressed Bob most about the McEwans was their garage and the three Packards that filled it. "They had a 1934 black Super Eight sedan, 1936 Packard Twelve victoria in yellow, and a 1939 One Twenty business coupe in black, for Mrs. McEwan."

Each November, Morristown Packard picked up the Twelve, put it in a DL & W box car, and shipped it to Florida for the winter. According to Bob, the McEwans spent every winter at the Breakers in Palm Beach.

In 1941, the business coupe was traded in on a new One Twenty station wagon for Mrs. McEwan, and Mr. McEwan ordered the 1942 Darrin victoria. His order was one of the earliest, and he received the first chassis off the 1942 line, fitted with the #1 1942 Darrin body from Hess and Eisenhardt. The hand-painted white letters *2001* on the right front frame rail and the left rear frame rail stand as mute testimony to this fact.

The car was ordered in Miami Sand with a Maroon Haartz cloth roof and red interior, and it was equipped with a short-wave radio, the K-steering wheel, automatic electric clutch, overdrive, directional signals, and backup light.

Although their cars were routinely traded in for new models, McEwan kept the stately 1936 Packard well into the 1950s. "When it was sold I can't recall," says Turnquist, "but I do know it is now in the state of Washington and has been fully restored."

The 1934 Super Eight sedan and the 1939 One Twenty business coupe wound up on Morristown Packard's used car lot in Irvington, New Jersey, some 20 miles away. Morristown Packard maintained its used car lot in Irvington so their customers in Morristown would not see their used cars driven by the parvenu! "The 1934 Super Eight sold for $100," recalls Turnquist.

Mr. McEwan requested that the Darrin be delivered on New Year's Day. The vehicle delivery plate was stamped January 1, 1942. "The McEwans had come back from Florida for the holidays and delivery of the Packard," recalls Turnquist. "They decided to have a small afternoon party in celebration of its arrival. New cars were a major purchase in those days, and often cause for a festive occasion. My parents were invited because of their mutual interest in gentleman farming. When we arrived, the car was parked in the driveway with admiring guests standing all around. It was beautiful. Simply breathtaking. The fact that it was a Darrin meant nothing to me at the time. In fact, it wasn't until the late 1940s that different coachbuilders became part of my vocabulary."

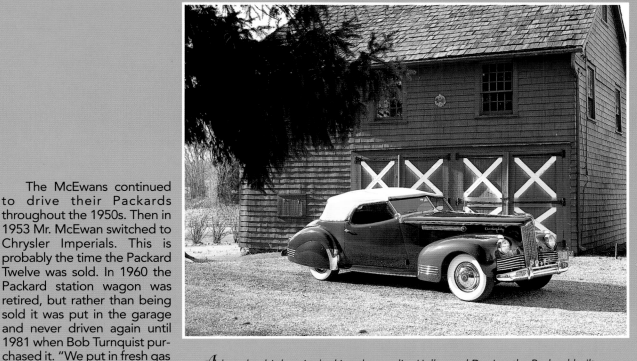

Although a bit heavier-looking than earlier Hollywood Darrins, the Packard-built semicustom Darrin victorias were nonetheless distinctively different from production Packard Super Eight victorias. The design was so popular that several cars duplicating Darrin styling were produced by independent coachbuilder Bohman and Schwartz in Pasadena, California, which copied the convertible sedan and victoria in 1941. In 1940 Rollson produced a Darrin-style victoria as well.

The McEwans continued to drive their Packards throughout the 1950s. Then in 1953 Mr. McEwan switched to Chrysler Imperials. This is probably the time the Packard Twelve was sold. In 1960 the Packard station wagon was retired, but rather than being sold it was put in the garage and never driven again until 1981 when Bob Turnquist purchased it. "We put in fresh gas and made a nonstop trip to Baltimore without missing a beat. The 1941 Packard station wagon had been replaced by a 1960 Dodge station wagon. That car now sits in the field rusting away."

The Packard Darrin was probably retired in 1961— the year of the last inspection sticker on the windshield. Bob says that the car was placed in the garage, and that is where it remained until 1981, when he finally purchased it.

"Since 1946, when I returned from the service, I mentally had a spot in my garage for the Darrin. However, I didn't approach the McEwans until 1961 about selling the car. I felt that if they said yes, I wouldn't have enough money. When I did finally ask them, their answer was no, but if they ever decided to sell, I could buy it. That was encouragement; however, as it turned out, selling old cars was the farthest thing from his mind," said Turnquist, recounting the incredible tale of financial misfortunes that befell McEwan in the 1960s.

"Mr. McEwan's friendly family stockholders sold the mills out from under him. Two years later he took in a young partner to help run the railroad. Through a series of devious maneuvers, the young man got control of the company, and within two years the once-successful Morristown Erie Railroad was bankrupt and the young man was facing criminal charges. All of this had a disastrous effect on Mr. McEwan's mind. One day he wandered off into the woods and they eventually found him sitting under a tree at the far end of his property. He was placed in a nursing home where he eventually passed away at age 79.

"Mrs. McEwan visited the nursing home every day to care for his personal needs. On several occasions she asked if she could sell the Darrin to me, and he would always say no. Mrs. McEwan told me that in retrospect, selling the Packard to anyone represented his reaction to someone trying to take away another prized possession.

"Once a year I would visit with her and we would talk about selling the Darrin and the station wagon in the garage. She would say to me, 'Sharpen your pencil, Robert!' Then one summer day in 1981, she called and said she wanted me down immediately to buy the cars. I told her I would be there in 35 minutes. I arrived 10 minutes late. Now remember, she is 81 years old at the time, and she says, 'Where were you, stuck in heavy traffic?'"

After years of being told no, Bob was curious as to the reason for the sudden change of heart. "I asked her why she was in such a hurry to sell them, and she replied that every time the caretaker would open the garage doors to get a tool, a passerby would see one of the cars, drive in and ask if they were for sale. She found this problem very unnerving.

"After restoring the Darrin, I drove over to Mrs. McEwan's house and asked her if she would like a ride, but got the usual no. Over the years, I would occasionally stop by to say hello, and on one occasion she allowed me to go through her husband's personal files to look for car pictures. There was not one car picture of any description to be found." Whatever importance these cars had held for Richard McEwan, it resided solely within the man, and when he died, so too, did their meaning.

Said Bob of this stunning example of classic sporting elegance, "We who own classic cars rarely know the original owners, let alone know them personally. I was lucky!"

The master of illusion, and arguably one of the greatest automotive designers of the twentieth century, Howard "Dutch" Darrin was honored in the 1970s by General Motors. Darrin is pictured in front of photographs showing some of his greatest designs with Tom Hibbard, Fernandez, and Packard. Behind his right shoulder is a photograph from his polo-playing days in France, and to the far top right, a Kaiser-Darrin sports car. *Dave Holls collection*

with the first several cars. The Hollywood Darrins were also fitted with the custom-built windshield frames and Dutch's favorite modification—cutdown, suicide-style doors.

Darrin interiors remained generally stock with the exception of a padded dashboard, a design favored by Dutch not only for its handsome appearance but inherent safety. Well ahead of its time, the Darrin padded dash extended across the entire width of the driver's compartment and continued around into the tops of the doors, giving driver and passenger a soft armrest with the windows lowered.

"The very early cars," said Stoessel, "were not like the later ones we did on the Sunset Strip. The first two still had running boards. We built one for Clark Gable and another for actor Chester Morris. The first two cars also lacked the cast-aluminum cowl and were fitted with handmade wood-frame cowls."

Once production got underway on the Sunset Strip, there were usually six cars being built at any given time. Stoessel had it worked out so that his staff could turn a standard Packard coupe into a Darrin victoria in just two weeks.

Even though only 16 custom-bodied Packards were produced at the Sunset Strip shop between 1937 and 1939, it seemed as though everyone in the Hollywood film colony was driving one. Production of the original Hollywood Darrins concluded at the Sunset Boulevard shop in 1939. Although he was making a modest profit, Darrin wanted East Grand Boulevard to get involved with the production and sales of Darrin Packards, and by 1939 Dutch had parlayed the popularity of his cars into a sales pitch to Packard boss Alvan Macauley, to convince him that the custom-bodied specials were just what dealers needed to attract more showroom traffic. In typical Darrin fashion, he also solicited the backing of West Coast Packard dealers and slipped a 1938 One Twenty victoria onto the Packard Proving Grounds so it was right under the noses of sales representatives attending the annual dealer show. For Darrin, the deal was almost *fait accompli* when Macauley arrived.

For the 1940 model year, Darrins appeared in the Packard catalog for the first time and were also used in Packard advertising. The first advertisement for the new Darrin sport sedan was in *Fortune* magazine. An ad for the convertible victoria followed in the *Saturday Evening Post*, with bold copy that hailed the new model as "Glamour Car of the Year! (Of course, it's a Packard!)." The 1940 sales catalog listed three Darrin models: convertible victoria, convertible sedan, and the luxurious four-door Darrin sport sedan.

Darrin arranged to have the 1940 models built at the old Auburn automobile assembly plant in Connersville, Indiana. Around 50 victorias were built, a dozen convertible sedans, and three sport sedans. In the overall scheme of things automotive, a small number of cars, but with the Darrin name, each was a rolling advertisement for Packard styling that could not be overlooked. Darrin had built an image car that was worth more to Packard in prestige than in sales. Like Dutch himself, the cars bearing his name seemed larger than life and couldn't help but attract an inordinate amount of attention. In the early 1940s this was as good as it could get for Packard and for Howard "Dutch" Darrin, who would lead East Grand Boulevard into the 1940s with an all-new design known as the Clipper.

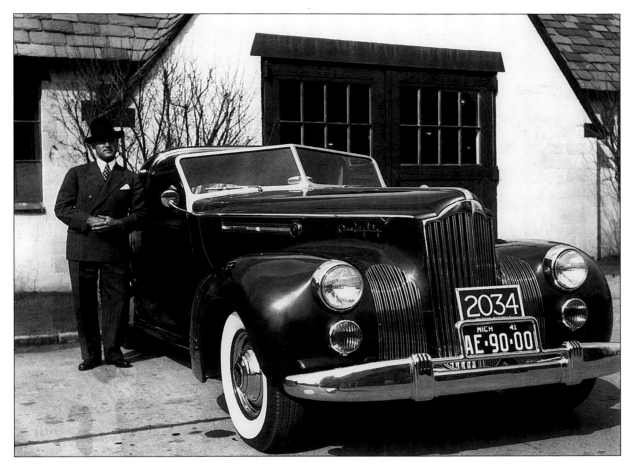

*I*n 1941 Ed Macauley had a Darrin-styled victoria modified into a landaulet by Hess and Eisenhardt. Known as the Phantom, the car evolved through several design evolutions at Packard until it finally became a Clipper-styled body in 1946. The removable plastic roof section covering the front compartment was designed by John Reinhart, who became Packard's chief stylist after the war.

Seven

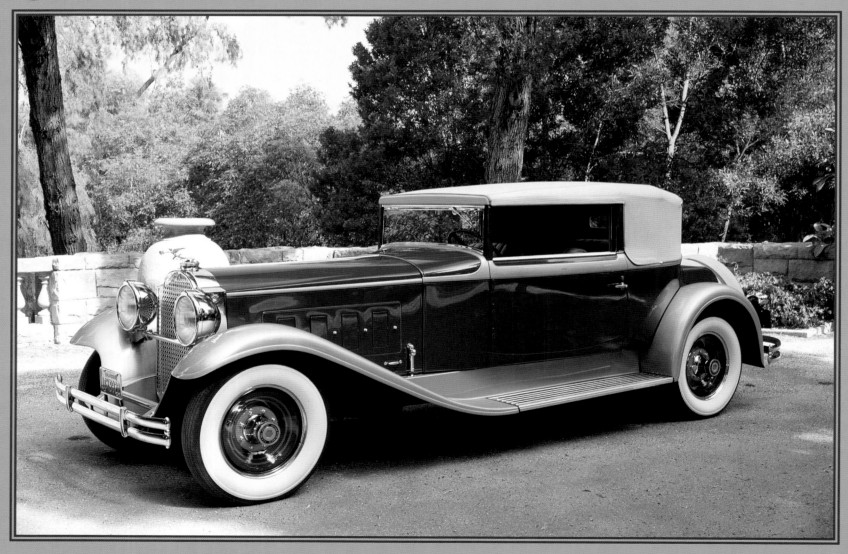

$\mathcal{P}$ackard $\mathcal{A}$broad

EUROPEAN COACHWORK

The Great Depression set the beat of the 1930s to metronome-like efficiency, marking the decline of annual automobile sales and the predictable demise of luxury auto makers. Reality finally struck Packard in 1934. Calendar-year sales declined from an all-time high of 47,855 in 1929 [1] to an abysmal 6,265.

Back in 1929, however, things looked far different. Packard had just introduced the new Seventh Series, a product of prosperity. The all-new factory-catalogued body styles, designed entirely by Ray Dietrich, had a flowing, almost sweptback appearance, highlighted by long, graceful fender lines and bold body garnish moldings. For the 1930 models there were three wheelbase lengths available: the 733 Standard Eight, with a 134 1/2-inch span; the 740 Custom Eight, measuring 140 1/2 inches; and the 745 DeLuxe Eight, with a 145 1/2-inch stretch. The 740 and 745 models were both equipped with Packard's 106-horsepower, 384.8-cubic-inch L-head inline eight, while 733 series models were powered by a smaller displacement 319.2-cubic-inch L-head eight producing 90 horsepower.

The cataloged coachwork for all three model lines was identical. In fact, the 5-inch difference in wheelbase between the 740 and 745 was not taken up by a larger passenger compartment as one might expect, but rather by a

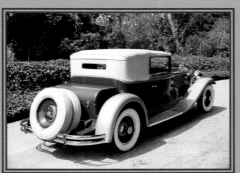

longer hood! For custom coachwork, Packard did offer a special Model 745 C chassis, which had the engine mounted closer to the radiator, thereby increasing the distance from the firewall to the center of the rear axle, adding nearly 5 inches to the length of the passenger compartment. The 745 C chassis were most often bodied as seven-passenger limousines. Packard listed six 745 C styles, with bodies by LeBaron, Rollston, and Dietrich.

The 1930s models were the last that Packard built using a single casting for the intake and exhaust manifold, and the first to offer Packard's new four-speed manual transmission. This was not a conventional four-speed by today's standards, offering a higher top gear, but rather the same three forward speeds as previously used, with an added *extra low* first gear.

Packard 745 models had a variety of distinguishing characteristics. They were the only models to have umber-colored dash knobs and a triangular radiator cap (along with the 734 Speedsters). Exclusive to the 745 models were hood side moldings embellished with a barbed spear head. The series also featured twin spare tires, either in the traditional side-mount location or on a double wheel carrier at the rear. The 745 was an ideal model for foreign coachwork, adaptable to a variety of continental styles. For the 1930 model year, a total of only 974 DeLuxe Eight 745

An inboard trunk and dual mounts, with the rear bumper beautifully shaped to surround the base of the spare tires, set this stunning French-bodied Packard apart from many of its American contemporaries. While it seems almost impossible to improve on the Dietrich victoria design, Maurice Proux managed to do just that in 1930.

OPPOSITE

*S*ubtlety was rarely a trait of French coachwork, but on this exquisite victoria bodied in the Paris atelier of Maurice Proux in 1930, the lines of a Dietrich victoria were handsomely altered to create a very formal convertible. Most significant are the uniquely shaped doors, which are lower in the center and extend out over the frame and running boards.

chassis were produced. Total Packard output for the same period was 28,386.

Although the repercussions of America's distressed economy would greatly decrease demand for costly custom-made cars throughout the 1930s, some of the finest body designs of the decade were being penned in Europe, particularly in France, where Packard was favored among all American makes, rated as highly by Europeans as the J Duesenberg and 16-cylinder Cadillac.

Packard records show that more than 20 foreign coachbuilders catered to the cars from East Grand Boulevard. In Great Britain, where a considerable number of Packard chassis were sold, coachwork in the British tradition was supplied by Barker and Company, Carlton Carriage Company, Freestone and Webb, Hooper and Company, H. J. Mulliner and Company, and Salmons and Sons.

In France, the renowned ateliers—Henri Chapron; Franay, which built an elegant Sedanca de Ville in 1939; Hibbard and Darrin, which produced several fine examples including a 1928 convertible sedan for American singer Al Jolson; Kellner and Cie.; Letourneur et Marchand; Maurice Proux; and

*T*he interior of this 1930 Packard by Letourneur et Marchand was completely hand-built and trimmed with walnut panels below the windshield and door windows. The woodwork was embellished with cast figurines of running silver foxes. The front seats were individually mounted, and on the long-wheelbase chassis, there was ample leg room for even the tallest driver. The interior featured twin gloveboxes, cigar lighter, and a Dragon-eye onyx shift knob on the four-speed gear selector.

Very French, very Bugatti, and very Letourneur et Marchand, this 1930 Packard Model 745 chassis was bodied for the Paris Salon. Take away the wheels and the grille and there is nothing to indicate that this is a Packard! The famed French carrosserie was known for its flamboyant styling, which was not lost on this victoria, distinguished by the unique placement of the door handles, stylish cycle fenders, louvered frame, polished step plates in place of running boards, and Stephen Grebel spotlight.

The Packard DeLuxe Eight was one of the most impressive engines of the 1930s. The L-head straight eight displaced 384.8 cubic inches, a bore and stroke of 3 1/2x5 inches, with an output rated at 106 horsepower. These bullet-proof, almost silent, engines could propel a coachbuilt model briskly up to 80 miles per hour. Even this aged engine runs almost as quietly and with equal agility as it did 68 years ago.

Baxter-Gallé—all designed and built a wide variety of town cars, victorias, phaetons, and Sedanca de Villes.

In nearby Belgium, the renowned house of Van den Plas was responsible for at least two Packard bodies. One, a 1926 Second Series Eight chassis bodied as a faux cabriolet, was the Grand Prix winner of the Nice-Cannes Concours d'Elegance that year.

In Germany, Glässer of Dresden (later known for producing Porsche 356 bodies in the 1950s) crafted a handsome convertible sedan, and Karosserie Neusse produced a rather severe-looking cabriolet on a Model 633 chassis.

Packards were also popular in Sweden. A Twin Six chassis was fitted by Hofslageribolaget with a very rakish roadster body in 1919, while Norrmalms coachworks of Stockholm bodied a 1928 Model 443 chassis as a convertible sedan and a 1928 Model One Twenty as a cabriolet. Gustav Nordbergs was known to have produced several formal town broughams and special tourers on the Packard Twin Six and Eight chassis. Finally, Graber of Switzerland built several custom Packard bodies in the early 1930s, particularly drop-head coupes (cabriolets and victorias).

Among several Packard chassis shipped to France in 1930 was a 745 delivered to Paris coachbuilder Maurice Proux. Along with an L-29 Cord town car, this is believed to be one of the few American cars bodied by the Courbevoie-Paris carrossier.

Proux actually combined parts from two 1930 Packards, the 745 chassis and a Standard Eight club sedan, attaching the chassis plates from both cars to the victoria. Proux bodied the car entirely out of steel, discarding the factory-supplied pieces and building his own fenders, hood, and cowl.

This car is perhaps one of the finest known examples of European coachwork on the Packard 745. Proux's fender styling was distinguished from Packard's by a tapered bead, which began at the inside front curve and trailed along the outer edge, with the reveal progressively getting thinner until it vanished at the head of the running boards. The hood also had more roll to its shape, as it came back from the stock radiator to the custom cowling.

The overall styling of this car could be considered conservative for a French designer, but truly elegant, almost formal in style and character for an otherwise sporty cabriolet. The broad doors featured a cut-down design that curved at the bottom, rather than being straight across. Aside from the Continental spares, in most other respects Proux followed rather traditional lines, though different enough in appearance to distinguish the body from factory coachwork.

The dash layout and instrumentation on the 1930 Packard were left as they were when they came from the factory, but all of the interior trim was redone by Proux in lustrous hand-rubbed walnut. One very subtle change was the use of European window regulators, which have exposed gear tracks on either end of the window framework.

It is believed that Proux built the victoria for exhibit at Cannes in 1930, after which the French Ambassador to Argentina took delivery of the car. As to the stunning silver-and-green color scheme on this lone example by Proux, it was copied from a 1930 Dietrich-bodied 745 convertible victoria, pictured in the Packard sales brochure!

A far more flamboyant approach to the 1930 Packard chassis was undertaken by Carrossier Letourneur et Marchand. It, too, chose the Model 745 as the canvas upon which to create a stunning portrait in steel. The striking French coachwork exuded an air of European elegance on the lengthy 145-inch wheelbase with a body design reminiscent of Bugatti and Hispano-Suiza. Like the Proux victoria, this car was also displayed at the 1930 Paris Salon, thus giving Packard prominent recognition by two highly regarded French carrosserie. The Packard distributor for France also had an elaborate exhibit of American and European-bodied models at the 1930 salon.

Packard had an active export program and was building both left- and right-hand-drive chassis for European delivery. Chassis and cars destined for export carried a "Packard" script at the front in the panel just above the thermostatically controlled radiator shutters. In the 1940s, Packard dusted off the same script die to produce emblems for the trunk lids of their new Clipper models.

Historian, classic car restorer, and collector Bill Snyder said that the Letourneur et Marchand Packard, which is owned today by his son Steve, originally left the 1930 Paris Salon in the hands of a wealthy Argentinean, who had the car repainted a gleaming solid black. As displayed on the Letourneur et Marchand stand, the Packard had been dark green.

Said Snyder, "Unusual interiors were very much 'in' at the time in European custom-built cars. Snakeskin, ostrich hide, and other exotic leathers were all used. The Packard was originally trimmed with natural red horsehide—which still had hair on it! Dark green piping matched the original exterior color."

The interior also had a rather decorative touch on the walnut panels below the windshield and door windows, which were embellished with figurines of running silver foxes. Front seats were individual, with ample leg room provided for even the tallest driver and passenger. Those sitting in the rear were not penalized by the long front seat track. Letourneur et Marchand designed "step down" compartments into the rear floor to provide more than the norm in leg room.

Just as Duesenberg had a dealer in Paris, so too did Packard, which through its French agent, M. Barbezat, maintained a good stock of parts, and as Bill Snyder notes, "was noted for going the extra mile to keep Packard owners happy."

Snyder contends that one of the reasons this exotic American car wasn't confiscated by the Germans during their occupation of France was that they wanted to maintain good relations with South American countries, ". . . and the Packard's owner was an influential Argentinean."

After the war the car was shipped back to Buenos Aires, where it remained for the next 20 years. It then passed into the hands of the original owner's nephew, and still in running condition—although with a few non-Packard parts added over the years—was used at his vacation home some 200 miles from Buenos Aires.

In the 1960s the car was finally offered for sale by a broker, who placed a small ad in the Packard Club's newsletter. The Letourneur et Marchand 745 was purchased by Bill Snyder and over the years has been completely restored to Concours d'Elegance condition, preserving for posterity this rare French-bodied Packard.

A Very British Packard

In 1938, a gentleman named Harry C. Hatch purchased a Packard Model 1605 Super Eight chassis which was then shipped to London and bodied in the style of a Rolls-Royce Sedanca de Ville by the renowned coachbuilding firm of Barker. That in itself is not so extraordinary; Harry Hatch, on the other hand, was.

The weather in Toronto was still very cold in March 1939, although that was probably not on Harry

Hatch's mind as he settled down on the verandah of his winter home in Palm Beach, Florida. Across the courtyard, Walter Bibby carefully wiped down the right front fender of the dark blue Packard limousine. Seeing his own reflection, he paused, noticing that his tie was slightly askew. He straightened it and then continued along to the side mount where he began polishing the brightly chromed Packard hub.

It was perhaps an odd task for a man of his position. Bibby was a respected member of the Ontario Provincial Police, but his job was to remain close to Hatch, and what better way than as the family chauffeur. Bibby was "on loan" to Hatch from the OPP. He was a distinguished, impeccable man, who also took care of the Barker-bodied Packard Sedanca de Ville in the same fashion.

Each winter, Hatch and his family traveled by rail from their exclusive Rosedale estate in Ontario, Canada, to the Florida retreat, and the Packard was driven down to meet them. Not always this particular Packard; Hatch consistently owned at least two at a time since 1923, but this year, the new car that he had specially built in England was his favorite, and Bibby, properly attired in a cream-colored Palm Beach uniform, was giving it his full and undivided attention.

*T*here are many great Packards still surviving from the 1930s, some of which are among the most valuable collector cars in the world, very rare examples of custom coachwork by LeBaron and Dietrich, but even they become less remarkable when compared to a single example like this Barker-bodied Sedanca de Ville.

*T*he plush Barker-designed passenger compartment could easily accommodate three along with two additional occupants in the jump seats. On the floor is an original copy of the March 1938 issue of *Fortune*, which featured an article on the car's original owner, Harry C. Hatch.

Hatch was halfway to the car when Bibby noticed him. There were no plans to go out, and he turned as if to ask. Hatch just shook his head and opened the back door of the car. He was looking for the copy of *Fortune* he had been reading the day before. It was there on the floor where he had left it. An issue he had long awaited. Beginning on page 68 was his story, the man behind one of the largest and most successful distilleries in the world, Hiram Walker-Gooderham and Worts Ltd. of Canada.

It had been five years since the repeal of Prohibition, and Hiram Walker managed to wedge itself into the third or fourth place in the $500 million U.S. liquor business, somewhere behind Distillers Corporation, Seagrams Ltd., and Schenly. But Hatch had more going for him than some of his competitors. Just prior to the repeal of Prohibition, he came vaulting across the U.S.-Canadian border and began construction of a new distillery in Peoria, Illinois. It was up and running by the middle of 1934. With the Prohibition era behind

A unique creation that is certainly one of the most impressive and interesting bodies ever to grace the classic Packard chassis, this very formal Sedanca de Ville was built by Barker of London, coachmaker to the Royal family, for Canadian liquor baron Harry C. Hatch. Owned today by noted Packard collector Richard J. Livoini, the stunning 1938 Model 1605 Packard Super Eight gives the appearance of being a Rolls-Royce limousine.

Known for building exquisite coachwork on European chassis, Van den Plas of Brussels, Belgium, executed this stunning faux cabriolet on a Second Series Packard Eight chassis in 1926 for Max Sauvau. The elegant Packard was entered in the Concours d'Elegance at Cannes in 1926 and won the Grand Prix (Best of Show) award. *National Automotive History Collection, Detroit Public Library*

On the way to foreign shores, a Packard chassis is loaded onto a freighter bound for Europe. Packard was to become one of the most popular American-made cars sold on the Continent throughout the 1920s and 1930s. *Department of Automotive History, Detroit Historical Museums*

him, Hatch began to expand Hiram Walker on an even larger international scale. His next and most ambitious venture was to build one of the largest distilleries in the world right under the nose of England's Big Five: Dewar, Johnnie Walker, Black and White, Haig and Haig, and White Horse. He also purchased a number of smaller English distilleries and became the exclusive importer of Ballantine Scotch. Not bad for a man who started out 27 years earlier with only $2,500 and a small liquor store in Whitby, Ontario. By 1937, Harry Hatch was one of the wealthiest men in Canada, and perhaps in the entire world of the late 1930s. Reason enough for a man like Bibby to be "assigned" to him. Harry Hatch was the most heavily insured citizen in Canada.

Hatch could have afforded any car in the world easily, yet he chose Packards. The family had owned at least 25 before Hatch purchased the Model 1605 Super Eight chassis and shipped it off to Barker in 1937.

On his numerous trips to England, he had become well acquainted with the House of Barker in London. It was one of England's oldest coachbuilding firms, established back in the eighteenth century as carriage maker to the royal family. In the age of the automobile, Barker became the premiere coachbuilder to Rolls-Royce. It was its well-known expertise in building luxurious motorcar bodies that brought Hatch to 66 South Audley Street in 1937. And none too soon, as it would turn out. With the decline in demand for specialized bodies and the rise in operating costs, Barker found it increasingly difficult to carry on. Shortly after the Packard Sedanca de Ville was delivered, the firm went into liquidation and was taken over by Hooper, ending a centuries-old concern that had been established in 1710 by one of Queen Anne's officers of the Guards. Such realizations put history in stark perspective. Barker was older than the United States!

This then is perhaps one of the last cars to be built by Barker and one of the few Packards ever to be bodied by the London firm. The styling is purely Rolls-Royce in almost every detail, save for the Packard grille. The stately Sedanca de Ville body was made entirely of aluminum and mated precisely with the Super Eight's 139-inch chassis.

Barker's dignified and traditional Rolls-Royce styling was exactly what Hatch wanted, a car that could have been built for royalty, and to that end, the craftsmen at Barker spared no expense. In keeping with its role as a chauffeured limousine, the car was simply enormous, especially when viewed from the rear, a perspective from which it easily could have been mistaken for a Rolls-Royce. The chauffeur's compartment was finished in black Connolly leather, sedately retaining all of the 1938 Packard fittings for the instrument panel. Aside from that, and of course, the Packard straight eight under the hood, the body was entirely custom built. The passenger compartment was abundant with special features: a built-in bar, twin lighted vanities, an intercom, a divider window, and a unique power-operated rear window shade that required a rather complicated mechanism consuming a small portion of the trunk. The trunk itself was a piece of work, fitted with two individual storage compartments, one of which was a solid steel, double-locked floor safe.

With all of its embellishments, the Sedanca de Ville weighed well over 2 1/2 tons, and even with the Super Eight's 135-horsepower engine, the car seemed underpowered and would take some time to reach speed. That wasn't to say the Super Eight

couldn't go fast. A later owner was once stopped for speeding at more than 85 miles per hour.

Over the years, the elegant Packard made innumerable trips from Toronto to Palm Beach, accumulating more than 80,000 miles. It remained in the Hatch family for 23 years. Even after Hatch passed away in 1946, at the age of 63, his wife continued to have the car driven to the Florida retreat each winter until the late 1950s. Such was the devotion of Packard owners on both sides of the Atlantic.

Packards were highly regarded in Europe, and at the major auto salons, there was always a strong Packard presence. This photograph from the Packard archives was taken at the opening of the 1931 Brussels show. Department of Automotive History, Detroit Historical Museums

The French preferred Packards over any other American car, with the possible exception of the Model J Duesenberg. The Packard representatives in Paris always made a grand showing at the annual auto salon, and here at the opening in 1930, the Packard exhibit is being reviewed by a gathering of French officials. Department of Automotive History, Detroit Historical Museums

Eight

The Proving Grounds

ASK THE MEN WHO TEST THEM

"You think that old back road is rough? You should see the chuck holes, sand pits, railroad ties, and water obstacles at Packard's 560-acre Proving Grounds north of Detroit—where it takes a crew of engineers just to keep the roads *bad!*" That was the opening paragraph to an article on the Packard Proving Grounds that appeared in the early 1950s.

The promotional piece, produced by Packard, noted that the car's ". . . built-in quality is proved on smooth pavements, too. The 2 1/2-mile concrete oval at this multimillion-dollar 'laboratory' is *the world's fastest closed track*, so beautifully banked that you can take a Packard safely around the turns at 100 miles an hour . . . *without even having your hands on the wheel!*"

Packard had built one of the most advanced testing facilities in the automotive industry with roads that duplicated conditions ranging from the steep hills of San Francisco to the Badlands of South Dakota, to the loose gravel and ruts of treacherous detours everywhere, ". . . in order to test and prove the quality of Packard design, engineering, and construction under every conceivable driving condition."

Test cars were subjected to as many as 50,000 torturous miles of the most grueling, abusive treatment imaginable in all kinds of weather: in hot, humid Michigan summers and freezing winters; in mud, snow, and

whatever else Mother Nature could throw at the Packard Proving Grounds.

Packard was one of the first American auto makers to build a test track, establishing the Utica Proving Grounds, located some 20 miles to the north of Detroit, in 1928. The idea had actually been considered by Packard management many years before, but the consensus was that in the early days of the motor car, America *was* a test track. Indeed, the roads from Detroit to Chicago, or New York, were a trial for any automobile in the early 1900s.

Paved roads were rare even in major cities, although in Europe paved roadways had been in use since 1816, when British inventor John MacAdam originated crushed stone pavement, which came to be known as "macadam." He later added tar to the surface binding the stones together to form "tarmac," which is still in use today as the most common road surface in the world.

Packard was finally moved to build the Proving Grounds in the late 1920s, after road tests had become more and more difficult to conduct in and around Detroit. Increasing traffic congestion, speed limits, and a raft of complaints from genuinely irritated citizens weary of Packard test drivers routinely applying brakes, accelerating away in traffic, and turning corners at breakneck speeds, encouraged East Grand to join the ranks of auto makers conducting vehicle evaluations in private.

Constructed in 1928, the Packard Proving Grounds had a complete garage facility for inspecting test cars. The bays were part of a striking Tudor-style estate house that served as a residence for the Proving Grounds manager, Charles Vincent, brother of Packard's legendary chief engineer and vice president, Colonel Jesse Vincent. *National Automotive History Collection, Detroit Public Library*

OPPOSITE

The Packard test track was four lanes wide with the corners banked at 35 degrees. It allowed production models to be driven at speeds of up to 100 miles per hour. *Department of Automotive History, Detroit Historical Museums*

Back in 1915, a year after establishing their Detroit company, the Dodge Brothers had built the city's first factory proving ground, consisting of a test hill and a small board track. Packard would actually have been the first auto maker in Detroit to build a testing facility, had the board of directors taken Henry Joy's advice.

From the time he discovered the cars of James Ward Packard in the late 1890s, Joy had been a visionary, bringing the Warren, Ohio, company to Detroit in 1903 and establishing the production and executive offices on East Grand Boulevard. In 1915 Joy marched into the boardroom to tell the directors that he had just bought land, which he explained could be used for construction of a testing facility. Their reaction was one of incredulity. Why should the company invest money in land to test cars, when the experience gathered from Packards being driven all around the country was more than sufficient to ascertain any shortcomings in the car's design? Undaunted, Joy mentioned that the facility could

also be used for another notion that intrigued him, the production of aircraft engines and airplanes. The board was still not convinced. The plan was rejected and Joy sold the land, which, ironically became the site of Selfridge Field, a U.S. Army Air Force base. As Joy had foreseen, however, Packard soon became involved in the aviation industry, manufacturing 12-cylinder Liberty aircraft engines during World War I. From that time forward, Packard would have an active aviation department, which decades later was to be the company's single most attractive asset when Curtiss-Wright came to the "rescue" of Studebaker-Packard in 1956.

Perhaps the greatest influence on Packard's decision to pursue the development of a testing facility was the opening of General Motors gigantic proving grounds at Milford, just 30 miles west of Detroit, in 1924.

Packard President Alvan Macauley found sufficient acreage in nearby Utica, and the company purchased its first 340-acre plot in 1925. The noted architectural firm of Albert Kahn Inc. was contracted to design and supervise construction of the Packard test site, the most important feature of which was to be a 2 1/2-mile oval high-speed track. For its time, it was a masterpiece of engineering. Noted James B. Forman, one of the men who would be employed at Utica, "The track was so perfectly banked that you could drive into the curve at either end full throttle (about 100 miles per hour) and take your hands off the steering wheel, and the banking would guide the car around the curve and onto the straightaway. The drivers liked to initiate the new people on the test crew by demonstrating this."

In addition to the track, Packard built a striking slate-roofed Tudor residence house for the Proving Grounds manager and his staff, maintenance shops, and testing laboratories. The road testing facilities, eventually expanded to 560 acres, included hills of varying gradations, plus mile upon mile of gravel, dirt, and sand roadways. The huge oval test track was four lanes wide, with the banked corners rising to a 35-degree slope at the center. It was the epitome of a

super highway for smoothness, whereas the off-road areas were the absolute antithesis, strewn with rocks, piled with sand, laced with muck holes, and one devilish, bone-jarring stretch comprised of railroad ties embedded crosswise at 1-foot intervals! There were hills at Utica steep enough to make Lombard Street pale, bumpy country lanes to tax suspensions and chassis, and 10 miles of hairpin curves. When a car left the Packard Proving Grounds, it had been over every imaginable kind of terrain.

On June 14, 1928, with the facility not yet fully completed, racer Leon Duray went to Utica to test the top speed performance of his Miller Special, and with it, the "speed of the track." In essence, the top speed of a race car is not only limited by the engine's capabilities, the gearing, suspension, and tires, but by the track on which the car is running—the design of the track surface, banking, and how much speed it can safely allow a car to obtain in the straights and corners.

Only weeks before, Duray had set a record with the Miller at the Indianapolis Motor Speedway, posting a top speed of 124.018 miles per hour. On the newly completed 2 1/2-mile oval in Michigan, he took the same car up to an astonishing 148.7 miles per hour to establish a new world's closed-course record and earn the title of "World's Fastest Speedway" for the Packard test track. [1]

The Packard Proving Grounds were under the direction of Charles H. Vincent, the brother of Packard's legendary chief engineer Colonel Jesse Vincent. Charlie had joined his brother at Packard in 1916, Jesse having been with the company since mid-1912. In the past, Charles Vincent had been a test driver and mechanic for Thomas-Detroit, shortly after the turn of the century, and later experimental engineer at Ferro Machine and Foundry in Cleveland and with Hudson in Detroit during Super Six development days. He was a well-trained, self-educated engineer. Vincent ran the Proving Grounds from its opening in 1928 and remained with Packard until 1947.

While he lived quite comfortably in the shadow of his famous brother, his job was perhaps more difficult. Years later Charles remembered that "Jesse was the genius who loved to create new things while I was the man who would make them work." A *Fortune* magazine writer once noted parenthetically that "Colonel Vincent's brother Charles . . . indulges a

Driving conditions in the 1930s often included flooded roads, and the Packard testing facility had its own manmade water crossing to test the car's ability to keep watertight. Water trials like this would dampen the ignition system—and spirit—of most any car, but Packards took one dunking after another without stalling. *Department of Automotive History, Detroit Historical Museums*

OPPOSITE

This section of the Proving Ground was known as "The Valley Road," a country lane that led to one of the steepest hills on the test circuit. *Department of Automotive History, Detroit Historical Museums*

People drive year round, so Packard tested cars the same way. In the dead of winter the off-road course became a different kind of challenge for Packard cars and test drivers. Here a 1935 sedan negotiates a grade along "The Valley Road." On the test track, slippery road conditions were tackled at speed to test traction and handling. *Department of Automotive History, Detroit Historical Museums*

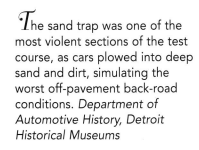

The sand trap was one of the most violent sections of the test course, as cars plowed into deep sand and dirt, simulating the worst off-pavement back-road conditions. *Department of Automotive History, Detroit Historical Museums*

This 1937 sedan has one wheel suspended off the road at the Proving Grounds to check structural integrity of the body. Department of Automotive History, Detroit Historical Museums

savage anxiety to find flaws in every Vincent creation," but Charlie was quick to note that "during the seventy-three years we were on this planet together, I do not think a harsh word ever passed between us."[2]

Charlie Vincent wasn't the only famous name attached to the Packard Proving Grounds in the 1930s. At his side was renowned Indianapolis 500 winner Tommy Milton, who joined Packard in April 1927. Packard paid him an impressive annual salary of $7,500—a figure indicative of his standing in the automobile field, his celebrity as a race driver, and his position as the number two man at the Proving Grounds. In years to come, Milton's signature on cars tested at Utica became a standard of excellence. For the first four years of its production, every Twin Six or Packard Twelve produced was driven 250 miles at the Proving Grounds in a break-in test that included maximum speed checks and a thorough inspection. The cars were then affixed with a "Certificate of

Approval" signed by both Vincent and the two-time Indy 500 winner.

Throughout the glory years of the Packard Proving Grounds, Charlie Vincent and his staff were allowed to pick cars at random from the factory shipping dock and reroute them to Utica. Under Alvan Macauley's edict, any new car or any new feature had to have Proving Grounds approval, in addition to an okay from Engineering and Distribution and other departments involved in the overall scheme of Packard production.

Whenever a new model was being introduced, at least five cars would be sent to the Proving Grounds to be driven 250 miles for operational evaluation and then thoroughly inspected for workmanship. Subsequently, one of them would be taken 1,000 miles for quality checking, both full throttle on the track, plus round after round on the off-road course. Another car might be subjected to 2,500 such miles, while still

108

What do you do when you can't find an elephant to sit on the roof? Pile enough sand bags on top of the car to compress the suspension, and then see if the doors open. Packard's did. *Department of Automotive History, Detroit Historical Museums*

another made to endure a full 25,000-mile test regime. On at least two occasions, a Packard was driven at top speed, day and night, for the seven days required to reach 15,000 miles, as effective as any performance and stamina test possible.[3]

There were three shifts of drivers to race each Packard test car on the track, which at one point in its history was averaging 1,078,125 test miles per year. During 1933 alone, the company reported test driving at Utica totaled 769,573 miles, a distance more than 30 times around the world at the equator.

Throughout the prewar history of the Packard Proving Grounds, no one was ever killed or injured. In 15 years, and millions of miles, there were, as Charlie Vincent stated, "no [serious] accidents. . . . During that same period GM had several men killed at their proving grounds. At one time while we were testing tires for Goodyear . . . one man drove steadily at top speed just to blow tires. He did this constantly for three months and never had any trouble when the tires blew."[4]

Charlie Vincent and his staff helped Packard maintain the highest quality standards in the American automotive industry throughout the 1920s and 1930s. The Utica Proving Grounds would go down in history as one of Packard's greatest assets.

During World War II, while Packard was engaged in the manufacturing of aircraft and marine engines, Chrysler built tanks. In need of a testing facility, Chrysler turned to Packard for help, and the patriots at East Grand decided to lease out the Proving Grounds for military use. This proved to be a costly error. By the end of the war, the once pristine concrete track surface was completely broken up by tanks and the off-road course all but flattened. The Utica Proving Grounds were nearly a write-off in 1945, but Packard was determined to reconstruct its legendary testing facilities.

*E*ven from 5,000 feet up, the world-famous Packard Proving Grounds looked plenty tough. *Department of Automotive History, Detroit Historical Museums*

The July 1947 issue of *Packard News* noted that management had reviewed three possible alternatives to repairing the badly damaged surface of the test track.

"First the entire track could be ripped up and a new one built. Second, the track could be merely resurfaced. But Roy Stougaard, head of Packard's Field Building and Real Estate Development, chose the third way of rebuilding the test track: resurfacing the test track first with a black material known as black-top and then covering that perfect black surface with a 6-inch slab of concrete."

The article continued, noting that, "A unique and forward looking engineering method was employed at this point. It has captured the interest of state highway commissions all over the U.S.A. and particularly the watchful eye of the Commission for the Design of Public Roads, Washington, D.C. For in this new Packard design only 10 contraction joints replace 230. . . . These 10 joints are entirely on the curves."[5]

The new concrete-over-blacktop process returned the high-speed oval to its former glory, and in October 1946 the Utica test track was reopened. It remained in use until Packard operations were transferred to South Bend, Indiana, in 1956.

Today, the Packard Proving Grounds are owned by Ford Motor Company, although they are no longer used for vehicle testing. The Classic Car Club of America holds an annual meet at Utica, and on those rare occasions when vintage Packards line the grounds near the old Tudor garages, if you listen carefully you can still hear the echo of straight eights and V-12s streaming around the ancient concrete oval.

Nine

The *C**lipper*

REDESIGNING THE PACKARD IN ITS OWN IMAGE

As Packard's director of design, Ed Macauley needed someone to come up with an all-new model for 1941. Macauley, who was the son of Packard chairman Alvan Macauley, surrounded himself with the best talent available outside of Harley Earl's Art and Colour Section at General Motors. In addition to Packard chief stylist Werner Gubitz (who had apprenticed under Ray Dietrich in the 1920s and joined Packard in 1930), he had John Reinhart (later to design the Continental Mk II for Ford), Phil Wright (designer of the 1933 Pierce-Arrow Silver Arrow), Howard Yeager, and Ed Nowacky.

Macauley's father and Packard's legendary engineer, Jesse Vincent, both suggested that he hedge his bet by going outside the styling studio to commission proposals from independent designers. Macauley engaged John Tjaarda and Alex Tremulis of the Briggs Body Company to work up a proposal of their own for a new model, along with independent designers George Walker (later of Ford Thunderbird fame) and Bill Flajole. This was a brain-trust that would have made any auto maker beam with pride, but Ed Macauley had one more name to draw out of his hat—Dutch Darrin.

Macauley contacted Darrin and offered him $1,000 a day if he could come up with a new design in 10 days. The reason for the sudden urgency, or the incredible amount of money offered, is not known. The irony of the thing, as Darrin lamented many years later, was that he never got paid for the design which he did in fact complete in 10 days. Since Packard was Darrin's largest client, there was very little he could do about it. Orders for Darrin Packards were increased as a kind of backhanded remuneration, and that would have been fine, but before they were put into production, Packard canceled the additional cars.

Darrin had a long-standing reputation for designing custom bodies that attracted attention, and what Macauley needed now was a production car that would do the same thing. Dutch gave it to him. Literally. Macauley came out to California, picked up Darrin's proposal in the form of a quarter-scale clay model, and took it back to Detroit. That was the last Dutch ever saw of it until the 1941 Clipper was introduced.

In a 1982 interview with the author, Briggs stylist Alex Tremulis recalled that when he first saw the clay model on display at Briggs he knew right away that Dutch had done it.

Custom coachwork was almost nonexistent by 1942, and Rollson built the last cataloged town car, and perhaps the very last custom Packard produced on the One Eighty chassis. The stately long 148-inch-wheelbase model was ordered by the Cory family (of coffee percolator fame) and delivered through the New York City Packard dealer on December 19, 1941.

OPPOSITE

With the introduction of the Clipper in 1941, Packard was headed in an entirely new direction, and models like this convertible coupe were fast becoming dated remnants of a fading era. By 1942 the only remaining examples of "classic" styling in the Packard line were the One Ten, now renamed the Packard Six and fitted with convertible-coupe coachwork, and the standard Packard Eight, also with convertible-coupe styling similar to this 1941 One Sixty.

"It had all of his characteristic touches, the downward swept beltline, a notchback roof flowing into a beautifully swept rear luggage compartment, and that rakish front fender angle Darrin so often used to accentuate Packard body lines," said Tremulis, drawing the shape of the car in the air with his hand, a telltale plume of cigarette smoke lingering for an instant where the roofline would have been.

While the Clipper is certainly Darrin's design, the car as it appeared in 1941 was the combined work of Darrin, Briggs, and Macauley's styling studio. Macauley turned the clay over to chief stylist Werner Gubitz and the design committee, which made some minor changes, ". . . vandalized it," claimed Darrin afterward, by shortening the front fender sweep so that it faded midway through the front door and raising the beltline, thus doing away with the stylish Darrin dip. Packard also decreased the size of the rear window, but the most offensive change to Darrin was the addition of running boards concealed by curved panels built out from the base of the doors and fenders. Darrin detested the use of running boards since the late 1920s. Yet even with these changes, the 1941 Packard Clipper looked fantastic. Dutch Darrin accomplished what no one had done for Packard in more than a decade: He created a car that was completely new, yet distinctively Packard.

A bold departure from traditional styling, the Clipper was 12 inches greater in width than in height, making it the widest passenger car then in production, and the Clipper's lower roofline was not at the expense of interior headroom. Just as GM designer Bill Mitchell had done to achieve a lower roofline with the 1938 Cadillac Sixty Special, the Clipper was built on a double-drop frame, which brought the floor pan closer to the ground, allowing interior dimensions to remain unchanged, yet allow a noticeably lower and sleeker exterior.

The Clipper's construction broke as much new ground as did the body styling. Unlike previous designs that had used separate pieces for much of the body, the Clipper's exterior panels were largely made up of individual stampings. The hood, grille, and each quarter panel (fenders) were formed from single sheets of steel. The entire roof was a single stamping from the windshield to the deck lid. The Clipper was also one of the first American cars to locate the battery under the hood, rather than beneath the front or

The Darrin-designed Packard Clipper was the best-styled car to come from Packard in years. Introduced as a single model in 1941, it was powered by the smaller Packard One Twenty engine. The 1942 models were offered in four lines, including the luxurious One Eighty Clipper touring sedan pictured.

rear seat, and to employ a floor-mounted starter switch, activated by turning on the ignition key and depressing the gas pedal to the floor.

Although they were originally powered by the smaller 282-cubic-inch straight eight used in the Packard One Twenty, Clippers were built on the 127-inch-wheelbase chassis normally reserved for the One Sixty and One Eighty models. A midyear car, Clippers did not start arriving in dealer showrooms until April 1941.

Only available as a four-door sedan, it was an immediate success. In the first year, which for the Clipper was shortened to only seven months, Packard sold 16,600 cars with a base price starting at $1,375. This represented a sizable percentage of 1941 model year sales, which totaled 72,855 cars.

The 1942 model year began in August 1941, and with it Packard expanded the Clipper line to include One Sixty and One Eighty series sedans, a new One Eighty fastback (designed in-house by Packard), and lower-priced Clipper Six and Clipper Eight models, built on a shorter 120-inch wheelbase. The only remaining examples of "classic" styling in the 1942

*T*he Clipper interiors, designed by Packard stylists, were beautifully detailed. Note the stylish door trim and woodgrained finish on the dashboard and door caps. Senior models had all-wool interiors, deep "Mosstred" carpets, and seven individual interior courtesy lights. There was a choice of four interior colors: tan, maroon, blue, or green.

*T*he Packard Super Eight One Eighty had one of the most powerful production engines available in America in 1942—Packard's 356-cubic-inch straight eight. With a bore and stroke of 3 1/2x4 5/8 inches, and a compression ratio of 6.85:1, output was a spirited 165 horsepower at 3,600 rpm.

Packard line were the One Ten, now renamed the Packard Six and fitted with convertible-coupe coachwork, and the standard Packard Eight, also with 1941 convertible-coupe styling. All remaining Packard models were Clipper designs, except for custom coachwork by Rollson and LeBaron and the semi-custom Darrin victorias.

The new One Eighty Clipper series offered one of the most powerful production engines available in America in 1942, Packard's 356-cubic-inch, 165-horsepower straight eight. One Eighty Clippers were treated to interior furnishings similar to Packard's older-style Senior models, including a choice of six tailored broadcloth upholstery materials, rear center armrest, wool carpeting, walnut-grained instrument panel and window trim, and a walnut-grained smoking set built into the front seatback.

The Clipper was the most stunning new car Americans had seen in years, but its future was doomed. The 1942 Packards had barely arrived in dealer showrooms when Japan attacked Pearl Harbor and Franklin Delano Roosevelt declared December 7, 1941, ". . . a date which will live in infamy."

In retrospect, World War II couldn't have been more damaging to any American auto maker than

Packard. The sleek styling of the Clipper was the best that East Grand Boulevard had offered customers since the late 1930s. Darrin's basic design and what Packard's styling department had planned to do with it throughout the 1940s might well have changed the course of Packard's future. At the beginning of the war there were plans to make the Clipper a complete product line that would include a convertible model (of which Darrin built one example in 1942 for his friend actor Errol Flynn) and a station wagon. Despite plans to continue building cars, on February 9, 1942, after selling more than 30,000 Clippers, Packard joined the rest of the American automotive industry in the war effort by suspending civilian automobile production. Had Packard produced Clippers for the entire 1942 model year, it is estimated that sales would have surpassed 80,000.

In addition to a new building to produce aircraft engines, the assembly lines at East Grand Boulevard were converted to the manufacturing of Merlin aircraft engines and 12-cylinder Packard marine engines to be used in PT boats built by Elco, Higgens, and Vosper, as well as Army and Navy rescue boats. To make way, Clipper tooling was

Among a number of changes Packard made to Dutch Darrin's original Clipper design was a two-tone paint scheme separating the roof and deck lid from the rest of the body. While this was generally an accepted practice in the 1940s, Darrin felt that it broke up the contour of the design.
Department of Automotive History, Detroit Historical Museums

Packard advertising for the new Clipper packed more into a page than almost any ad in the company's history, including the entire Packard price range, from $907 to $5,550. For the model year, Packard offered six lines of cars and 47 different body styles, but all the attention was going to the new Clipper sedans.
Department of Automotive History, Detroit Historical Museums

First streamlined car that considers the

ASK THE MAN WHO OWNS ONE

Brand-new addition *to the 1941 Packard line, now offering 41 body styles in 6 different model series. The sensational straight-* *eight Packard Clipper shown above is priced at only $1375* (not for just a coupe, but for the 4-door sedan illustrated).*

A YEAR AGO, Packard created a limited number of spectacular Custom One-Eighties. Prices: $4570 *and up*. They were a sensation! But could such a car be built in quantity, sold at a price? Packard engineers, style consultants, production experts put their heads together — produced a popular-priced car that outshone even its "parent", and brought a new idea to modern car design. This car is the new streamlined straight-eight you see at the left—the Packard Clipper.

The Clipper is more than a car with advanced streamline styling. It is *common-sense* design—the first car **to** recognize that *modern beauty* must be *functional* ... must serve *some useful purpose*.

Thus, every new feature of this lower, wider, roomier car makes a new contribution to the *safety, comfort,* or *convenience* of the passengers.

LOWER—FOR SAFETY—Low, rakish, the Clipper hits a new high in beauty. Its lower center of gravity also makes it a *safer* car. And thanks to the widest body on any car (the Clipper is *wider than high* by almost a foot!), "3-in-a-seat" room is much greater ... with no increase in overall car width!

FADE-AWAY FENDERS—This handsome new treatment bridges, *beautifully*, the long "between fenders" space that mars the looks of other cars. And letting the fender "fade" into the front door also results in more room *inside the body*. Running boards (concealed, of course!) are amply wide for safety.

HEADROOM IN BOTH SEATS—Modern design gives the Clipper not only a far more graceful rear contour, but something hitherto absent in streamlined cars—full headroom in the *rear* seat as well as the front. Note, too, that even the *rear* fenders are seamless—blended smoothly into the body.

NEW EVEN TO THE "RIDE"!—This streamlined Clipper is an engineering masterpiece from the road up. For example: the Clipper's new Air-Glide Ride is just as sensational, just as new as its styling! Cradled in a newly-designed spring suspension, the Clipper levels out the roads with a magic ease—and it's the first car that gives *rear-seat* passengers all of the comforts of a "front seat ride".

All told, there are 84 exciting new advancements wrapped up in the Packard Clipper—and every one of them is a good reason for dropping in at your Packard dealer's *right away!*

National defense work comes first with Packard!—Marine motors for the Navy, and Rolls-Royce aviation engines for the Army, have the clear right-of-way. But Packard is big enough to handle its defense assignments and car production—so important to employment and prosperity—at the same time.

6 lines of cars—41 body styles

$907 TO **$5550**

Delivered in Detroit—white sidewall tires and State taxes extra.

Prices subject to change without notice.

sheathed with cosmoline, covered with tarpaulins, and sent to open storage. Throughout the war, most of the machinery needed to manufacture the Clipper sat out in the weather.

During the war, Packard sold the tooling for the older-style cars of the Seventeenth, Eighteenth, and Nineteenth Series to the Russians, one of the reasons so many postwar Soviet-built ZIS[1] staff cars looked like late 1930s Packards. They were. For the men of East Grand Boulevard there now loomed a great problem; with only one remaining model, the Clipper, Packard faced a painfully slow return to production after the war. It took more than 12 months to get all the machinery cleaned and back into working order, and the assembly plants reconverted to automobile manufacturing. Packard still managed to build 42,102 cars in 1946 for the 1946 and early 1947 model years despite labor strikes and material shortages, which further hampered East Grand Boulevard's start-up of production.

Recalling the early postwar years, Packard's chief plant engineer, Dick Collins, remarked that the con-

dition of the Clipper tooling was deplorable. "We'd bring in machines, and the motors and electric controls all had to be overhauled." Despite the precautions taken in 1942 to weatherproof the equipment, after almost four years of exposure, moisture got into everything. The government reimbursed Packard for the repair costs, but as Collins later said, ". . . the time required was what got us down. We really didn't get rolling until '47 or '48."[2] Unfortunately, by 1948, Packard was rolling in the wrong direction.

At the same time East Grand Boulevard was being cleaned up from the war, Packard began construction of a new final assembly line, which was hastily completed at the end of 1945. Finally capable of the production capacity Packard President George Christopher proposed in the early months after the war—roughly 200,000 cars a year—Packard launched its new Twenty-Second Series in the summer of 1947, replacing the original Clipper design with the amorphous bathtub styling of the 1948 models.

John Reinhart, Packard's new chief stylist, remarked that the company could have continued

A production Packard Clipper takes the rough road at the Proving Grounds in 1941. The cars were put through rigorous testing to evaluate the new chassis and front suspension design. *Department of Automotive History, Detroit Historical Museums*

The Proving Grounds had an extensive back-road course full of dips, and driven at high speeds, it was guaranteed to test the rebound of Packard's new Clipper suspension. And yes, that is three out of four wheels off the ground and the driver's head completely out of view! *Department of Automotive History, Detroit Historical Museums*

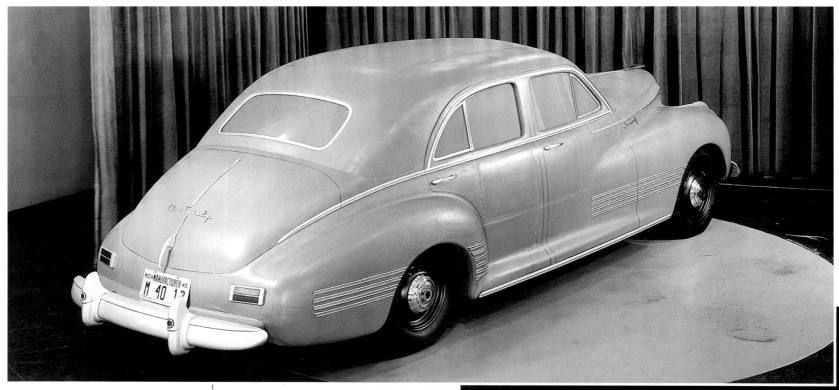

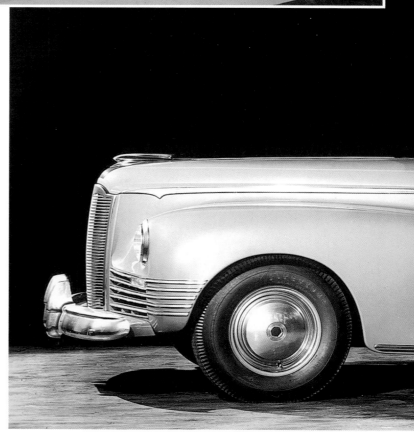

A full-scale model of the Clipper in the Packard styling studio sometime in 1940. In this proposal, chrome trim from the front fenders was repeated along the lower portion of the body. Fortunately, that idea never made it out of the studio. *Department of Automotive History, Detroit Historical Museums*

An early Packard studio photograph of the 1942 Clipper. The grille lines proposed on the 1940 prototype made a slight reprise on the 1942 models, wrapping around the front fender to the wheel opening; rear fender skirts were optional. *Dave Holls collection*

the original Clipper design for another two years with minor styling revisions, and it would have been a much better-looking car than the 1948 Packards.

While a truer statement was never made concerning the Twenty-Second Series, the Clipper was nonetheless a prewar design, and Americans wanted something brand spanking new in the jubilant postwar era. There was also considerable pressure on Packard management to compete with General Motors' top luxury models, and then there was Lincoln and Chrysler to consider, along with new designs from competitive independent auto makers like Studebaker and newcomer Kaiser-Frazier. Lamented Reinhart, "All of us at Packard styling wanted to advance the Clipper design, but instead management made a decision to reshape the car entirely." Concluded authors George Hamlin and Dwight Heinmuller in the award-winning book *Packard—A History of the Motor Car and the Company*, "It was unfortunate that the Clipper, born with such great promise, died as it did, a warmed-over prewar car, its freshness and impact destroyed by a four-year hiatus, spending its last model year making time for the face-lifted 1948 cars to come."

In the end, perhaps Dutch Darrin had the last laugh. The 1948 models turned Packard on the road to ruin, while the 1941 through 1947 Clippers became the last Packards recognized as *Classics* and the first postwar models to achieve *Milestone* status. They were at once the end and the beginning of an era. The right cars at the right time, albeit for too short of a time.

Ten

Postwar Packards

THE LAST AND THE BEST AND THE WORST OF TIMES

In the fall of 1945, every automotive designer in America was thumbing a pencil against a blank drafting table and wondering out loud, "What do we do now?"

"What do we do now?"

Somewhere in space those words are still floating around, echoing in the vast unknown along with radio waves carrying FDR's Fireside Chats and Milton Berle's first television broadcast on NBC. For Detroit, the war was over and assembly lines that had produced tanks and aircraft were coming to a halt. The time had come to get back to the business of designing automobiles, new automobiles for a car-starved country with money in hand and plenty of empty garage space.

While we tend to think of the prewar 1940s as a continuation of the classic styling that had dominated American design throughout the 1930s, the classic look was all but gone by 1941. Virtually every new automobile in the country had swept-through fenderlines and rounded envelope body styling. The best-looking of all, however, was the Packard Clipper, with a design that had truly broken new ground in automotive styling and construction, a watershed that few had the opportunity to appreciate before it languished and aged in the shadows of a world war.

In the early 1940s, Packard had seen several changes in its executive suite, the most drastic of which was the resignation of Max Gilman, who had assumed the position of president and general manager in 1938, when Alvan Macauley moved up to the chairmanship of Packard. In April 1942, however, Gilman had been caught having an affair with the wife of one of Packard's advertising managers, and in the 1940s, at Packard, this was considered rather bad form. Macauley asked East Grand Boulevard's number two man to step down, replacing him with George T. Christopher, a man who had risen within the company ranks through his ability to manage production. He had come to prominence after turning East Grand Boulevard's dated assembly lines into the most efficient operation in the company's history with the production of the Packard One Twenty. Christopher was also the man who had never cared for, as he once described it, all that "goddam senior stuff."[1] Thus with Christopher leading Packard into the postwar era, East Grand Boulevard was in for a change.

Packard had made a strong comeback with the Clipper in 1946 and 1947, giving the cars a mild face-lift to distinguish them from the prewar models. In 1946 that was about all any auto maker could do, and the public was willing to accept it. In fact, anything with four

---

As Clipper styling evolved in the postwar era, Ed Macauley's personal car, known as the Phantom, was used to test new ideas. This photograph was taken in August 1948 and shows a 1944 experimental front end combined with the 1948-style fender treatment. The Darrin-style door was still being used, as was the special roof that had been with the car since 1941. *Dave Holls collection*

OPPOSITE

The luxury flagship of the Packard line in 1946 was the Custom Super Clipper seven-passenger sedan (pictured) and limousine. The 1946 sales brochure noted that "Packard distinction is magnified in the Custom Super Clipper Sedan for seven passengers. Its completely new body combines lordly dimensions with superlatively fine custom treatment of detail."

125

Could these have been the cars that inspired the Russian government to purchase Packard's tooling during World War II? Perhaps. The last two 1942 Packards to sell were purchased by the Russian government and said to have been delivered to the Soviet embassy in Washington, D.C. Both were Super Eight One Eighty seven-passenger touring sedans bodied by LeBaron. *National Automotive History Collection, Detroit Public Library*

wheels and a new title sounded good in 1946 and 1947. If you wanted a new car, you either knew someone in the business or your name ended up at the end of a very long waiting list. There were no discounts, and there was no bargaining. With such favorable conditions, Packard could have sold more Clippers than it did in the first two years after the war, if East Grand Boulevard could have built them.

At the same time, Ed Macauley was overseeing the development of a new model for 1948 that was being designed at Briggs. Following George Christopher's dictate, the new car was to be an inexpensive rework of the Darrin-based Clipper. What Packard ended up with was a heavy-handed face-lift that extended all the way back to the rear deck lid. It was as if the stylists at

Briggs had stuffed an air hose up the tailpipe of a 1947 Clipper and blown the car up like a balloon.

While it is hard to believe that any design could prove unpopular in the late 1940s, the Twenty-Second Series was less than revered by the American automotive press, which lampooned the new models in print, pinning them with unattractive nicknames like "Bathtub," which, unfortunately for Packard, stuck like a dirty soap ring.

Although many people, including the majority of Packard stylists, did not like the new design, others proclaimed it one of the best-looking cars of the year, and 1948 models were heaped with international design awards, and record sales. In 1948 Twenty-Second Series Packards won the "Fashion Car of the Year" award from the Fashion Academy of New York; accolades as the "Finest and most beautiful car in the show," at Cacuta, Colombia; and the Concours d'Elegance prize from shows in Caracas, Luzerne, Sofia, and Monte Carlo. If not bemused by all this, then bewildered, Packard's chief stylist John Reinhart, who had replaced Werner Gubitz in 1947, summarized the Twenty-Second and Twenty-Third Series models as having "been in tune with the times, but not very attractive." No one, however, slammed the car as hard as legendary auto writer Tom McCahill, who lambasted the 1948 Packard with the nickname "goat."

Whether you like the car or not, it was still unmistakably a Packard. At the front there was a new squashed-down grille and reprise of the Packard family crest, and head-on the cars looked very stylish. In profile, however, the sedans and coupes looked like big jellybeans with an ungainly, bulbous hoodline. By the time you added the Packard hood ornament, the car looked like something had roosted on a knoll. The only saving grace was the Super Eight and Custom Eight convertible victoria. The convertibles, and then only with their tops down, were the lone saviors of Packard's early postwar designs.

Model lines for 1948 were comprised of the Chassis 2220 with only the six-cylinder engine available. Unfortunately, you had to own a taxi service to

buy one. The Chassis 2240 six was offered only for export and as a taxi cab. Within the eight-cylinder family there were eight model lines: 2201 offered in a four-door sedan, station sedan, and club sedan; 2211 DeLuxe Eight, available in a four-door sedan and club sedan; 2202 Super Eight, offered with the aforementioned body styles; the sporty 2232 Super Eight convertible; the 2222 Super Eight long-wheelbase chassis, bodied as a seven-passenger

Packard had the advantage of having Clipper styling in the early postwar years, which had been ahead of General Motors, Ford, and Chrysler in 1942. With a minor face-lift, East Grand Boulevard put the Clipper back into production in 1946, stating that the car, ". . . represents modern streamlining in its most advanced form." True in 1942, but less so four years later. *National Automotive History Collection, Detroit Public Library*

Packard was trading on its history in 1947 with press releases and staged photos such as this one from September 28, 1947, which stated, "Packard's traditional grille lines, which originated in 1904, are not only preserved but enhanced by the 'free flow' styling of the three all-new Packard Eights for 1948. Actually part of the front end design, the grille on the Eight (Touring Sedan shown here), the Custom Eight, and the Super Eight protects the radiator from damage, besides admitting cool air. The air also enters through the front bumper, whose long arms reach almost from wheel-opening to wheel-opening."

*I*n profile, the victoria looked better than any other 1948 Packard. Well worth the $1.5 million East Grand Boulevard had spent to develop its first postwar convertible models. Owned by Dan Sommer, this is one of the finest examples extant of the Twenty-Second Series Custom Eight convertible victoria.

sedan or limousine in standard or DeLuxe versions; the 2206 Custom Eight, a more luxurious version of the four-door sedan and club sedan; the top-of-the-line 2233 Custom Eight convertible victoria; and 2226 Custom Eight long-wheelbase limousines and seven-passenger sedans.

With the various series, there were a total of five wheelbases, four engines, and eight body types. The least expensive Packard was the Model 2295 club sedan at $2,250. The highest priced 1948 Packard was the Custom Eight long-wheelbase, seven-passenger limousine, boasting an f.o.b. window sticker of $4,868.

The foundation of the Packard line was the Standard Eight offered in traditional club sedan,

four-door sedan, and a brand new model designed to compete with Ford and Chrysler "woodie" station wagons, Packard's shapely station sedan, which had been built at the prompting of Ed Macauley. As it turned out, the new model offered few of the advantages one associated with station wagons and all of the inconveniences possessed by wood-appliquéd models of the late 1940s. The station sedan lasted through the Twenty-Third Series for 1949–1950 and then quietly faded from the automotive scene.

The DeLuxe Eight line for 1948 offered two- and four-door sedans, as did the more expensive Super Eight series. The gracious step up to the Super Eight gave purchasers a unique model complete with an

New Golden Anniversary Packard Eight, 135-HP Club Sedan—$2224—delivered in Detroit, state and local taxes, if any, and white sidewalls ($21), extra.

YOU'LL THINK THE FUEL-GAUGE NEEDLE IS STUCK!

Owners tell us there's one slow thing about the new Golden Anniversary Packards—the way the fuel-gauge needle creeps from "F" to "E"!

Thanks to Packard "free-breathing" engine design, the more powerful new Packard eights deliver gas mileage that's the sensation of the fine car field. And all the while, they'll delight you with silent *smoothness* such as you've never known. Sample it soon!

This you can BANK on! Gas mileage is HIGH. And service needs are LOW . . . lowest in our history…because this is the most durable Packard ever built. Quality note: Of all the Packards built, in the last 50 years, *over 50%, are still in service!*

New silence, too! Packard delights you with a new kind of scientific soundproofing—of body, engine, and chassis. For still greater comfort, Packard cradles this roomy interior with a costly "self-controlling" suspension system.

And here's the new drive sensation—*Packard Ultramatic Drive* . . . the *last word* in automatic, no-shift control. More *positive*, more *flexible*, more *responsive* than any automatic drive you've ever known! Get the story at your Packard dealer's!

Golden Anniversary PACKARD   Ask the man who owns one

135-HP EIGHT • 150-HP SUPER • 160-HP CUSTOM

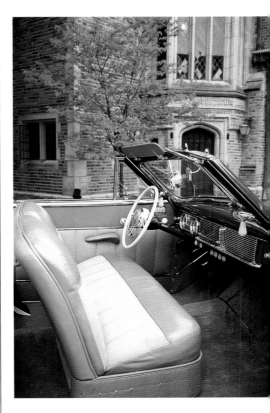

The 1948 Packard interior was well appointed. The linear chrome strip theme of the lower grille was repeated in the dashboard design, which features a vertical radio with station-selector buttons. Chrome was served up wholesale throughout the Packard interior, giving the cars a very luxurious appearance.

This 1949 advertisement publicizes Packard's fuel efficiency, comfort, and Ultramatic Drive transmission. It also calls attention to the company's golden anniversary.

exclusive 327-cubic-inch, 145-horsepower eight-cylinder engine, special 120-inch-wheelbase chassis, and the availability of a third body style, the convertible victoria. This positioned the Super Eight line (and companion long-wheelbase seven-passenger line[2]), midway between the lower-priced Packard coupes and sedans and the exclusive Custom Eight Series.

In July 1947, the Chassis 2232, Model 2279 Super Eight and Chassis 2233, Model 2259 Custom Eight convertible victorias were the first new models to be introduced. The flagships of the 1948 model line, Packard spent more than $1.5 million on tooling and engineering alone to ensure that there would once again be a convertible on showroom floors. The lack of a convertible model was the original Clipper's only real fault. Darrin built a custom for Errol Flynn in 1942, and it was every bit as dashing as the old Hollywoods. Rollson had also taken the cutters to a Packard, creating a similarly handsome Clipper convertible in 1942. No doubt, had the war not intervened, Packard would have followed suit.

With the new convertible models launched during an election year, Packard benefited from some free publicity when both President Harry S. Truman and Republican challenger Thomas Dewey chose Packard Custom Eights for their presidential campaign cars. Profiting from a strong new car market, Packard's campaign trail exposure certainly contributed to the Boulevard posting the second best sales year ever in 1948, with 98,897 cars built.

The Custom Eight line was Packard's most distinctive, differentiated from other models not only in price but in subtle design characteristics. At the top was the convertible victoria, selling at $4,295, making it the highest-priced Packard available in 1948, exclusive of limousines. A comparable Cadillac Series 62 convertible coupe, the glamour queen of the GM luxury line, was priced some $850 *less* than the Packard. In fact, the only Cadillac that cost more than a Packard victoria was the Fleetwood Seventy-Five limousine! Even Lincoln's exclusive 1948 Continental cabriolet, one of America's most expensive automobiles, commanded just $450 more than a Packard victoria.

The 1948 Custom Eight Packards were distinguished from other models by an egg-crate grille, a chromed egg-crate trim strip across the rear of the

car, a newly styled pelican (or cormorant, argue among yourselves) hood ornament, a double bar of brightmetal along the lower body panels, and traditional cloisonné wheel cover emblems.

Interiors were luxuriously appointed with Bedford cord and leather upholstery, cut-pile "Mosstred" carpets, duck down-filled seat backs and seat cushions, and, on convertibles, standard hydraulically adjustable seats and power windows.

Engines for the Custom Eight displaced 356 cubic inches delivering a substantial 160 horsepower via a column-mounted manual transmission. Packard continued to offer its Electromatic clutch option in 1948, a design considerably outdated compared to GM's automatic transmissions and the most obvious chink in Packard's new postwar armor. Well, that and the styling of the entire model line.

What Packard had dubbed its "Free Flow Styling" approach in 1948, which sounds much better than bathtub or goat, was about to flow on down the road just as the company celebrated its golden anniversary. The 1949–1950 Twenty-Third Series was a mildly face-lifted carryover of the Twenty-Second Series, and even though model designations

were shaken up with the Super Eight being kicked up a notch, this was hardly enough to commemorate half a century in the business. There was one highlight, however, the introduction of Ultramatic, the only automatic transmission ever developed by an independent auto maker up to that time, and one of the most successful designs of the postwar era.

As for Packard's 1948 through 1950 styling, it is what history best defines as a "successful failure." Enough people bought them to make it a success, and enough people hated them, including the majority of Packard dealers, stockholders, and board members, to make the Twenty-Second and Twenty-Third Series an albatross that would hang around George Christopher's neck. When the 1950 model year ended, the sales figures totaled 106,457 Twenty-Third Series cars, of which only 42,640 were 1950 models.

Packard failed to build the promised 200,000 cars a year, yet if it had, Packard dealers couldn't have sold them. Christopher left the water running in the bathtub too long, and Packard's profits were going down the drain.

It has been said that Christopher lost sight of the company's reputation for building luxury cars, but he

*H*ardtop coupes were very much in vogue and Packard joined in with a 1951 model, the first in the company's history. Packard was not among the Detroit auto makers to pioneer this handsome design, often referred to as a hardtop convertible, shown here in two different views. Both models have Ultramatic transmission, as noted by the rear fender script. *Department of Automotive History, Detroit Historical Museums*

The Twenty-Fifth Series models for 1952 bore little change. This August 1951 publicity photo shows the new hardtop. Packard management, first Christopher and then Ferry, had been bottom line since the 1948 models. Each year Packard moved further away from its roots. By 1952 the big 356-cubic-inch Custom Eight engine had been dropped and replaced by a nine-main-bearing version of the 327 rated at 155 horsepower. "Mosstred" carpets were no longer available; interior trim, particularly wood graining, was less abundant; and even the cloisonné emblems on the wheel covers were eliminated and replaced with painted emblems. It was, by all accounts, the cheapening of Packard. *Department of Automotive History, Detroit Historical Museums*

had never really liked them, having created Packard's first entry-level model in 1935. Instead, he continued to pursue the production of lower-priced models designed to compete with Buick, Pontiac, Ford, and Chrysler, rather than keeping pace with Cadillac and Lincoln. Hindsight perhaps, but in October 1949, under fire from stockholders and directors, Christopher retired from Packard. His legacy was a line of cars that had relinquished the Boulevard's last grasp on the luxury market.

The all-new Twenty-Fourth Series, introduced in 1950 as a 1951 model, saved the calendar year and put Packard back on a profitable path; but it was too little, too late. Packard lost too much prestige to Cadillac and Lincoln, particularly Cadillac, and was no

longer in a position to compete with GM's midpriced leaders, let alone a car that had earned a reputation as "The Standard of the World." If the convertible victoria was a bright spot in East Grand Boulevard's tarnished 1940s legacy, it was only a brief glimmer. The legions of owners who purchased cars in the early postwar years would not be back in sufficient numbers to save Packard in the coming decade.

Packard's history was in the production of great cars, not a great number of cars, and under the guidance of George T. Christopher, the men of East Grand Boulevard lost their direction and chose to follow a road less traveled. A road that for Packard was heading nowhere until James J. Nance arrived.

Eleven

The Road To Ruin

THE STUDEBAKER-PACKARD MERGER AND CARS OF THE 1950s

Sometimes, the best place to begin a story is at the end. The year was 1957 and America was nearing the end of a decade unlike any other, and the Packard, one of the world's oldest and most respected automobiles, was nearing its own end.

By the late 1950s, America had bid farewell to the age of innocence having survived its seasons of disparity—the Great Depression in the 1930s, the inhumanity of a second world war in the 1940s, followed by Korea, and the re-arming of peacetime America. We watched Senator Joseph McCarthy's televised witch-hunts for Communists, the birth of the nuclear power age with the launching of the submarine Nautilus, and the beginning of the U.S. Interstate Highway System under Dwight Eisenhower's administration in 1956. So many things changed in the early postwar years that Americans were practically spellbound. That sounds laughable by today's standards, when changes in world geopolitics and technology are so far-reaching each year, sometimes each month, that the 1950s seem dull in comparison. But back in those golden days of rock and roll, drive-in movies,

and tailfins, every change seemed breathtaking, especially those that took place in the U.S. automobile industry.

Today we have General Motors, which accounts for five original U.S. makes—Cadillac, Buick, Oldsmobile, Pontiac (originally Oakland), and Chevrolet (discounting GMC trucks and Saturn); Ford with a total of three—Ford, Lincoln, and Mercury; and then Chrysler bearing four brand names—Chrysler, Plymouth, Dodge, and Jeep. Of the latter, Chrysler inherited Jeep when it absorbed American Motors Corporation in 1987. Back in the postwar 1950s, however, the U.S. automotive industry was comprised not only of Ford, GM, and Chrysler (which at the time also consisted of DeSoto), but others as well. There was Hudson, Studebaker, Kaiser-Frazier, Nash, Willys, and Packard among the leading American manufacturers.

Although financially sound from its prewar years, Packard sales were abysmal. The re-introduction of the stylish Packard Clipper had only generated 42,102 sales for the 1946 and early 1947 model years. Packard's introduction of the 1948 Twenty-Second Series midway through 1947,

The original Pan American was based on a Twenty-Fifth Series Model 250 convertible. The car was sectioned 4 inches and otherwise lowered through the suspension. The hood had a functional air scoop, and the standard Packard grille had the outer bars shaved and mesh inserts added. The original paint scheme was Metallic Gold with top-grain Oyster White leather on doors, seats, center folding armrest, dash, and sun visors. The seats, door trim, and steering wheel had contrasting leather inserts. *National Automotive History Collection, Detroit Public Library*

OPPOSITE

The car that launched a brief and historic reprise for Packard in the early 1950s, the 1952 Pan American show car. The original car was built for the 1952 New York International Motor Sports Show where it was a sensation and won the show's top award, the Gold Trophy for Outstanding Design and Engineering Achievement. Formerly owned by the family of Alvan Macauley, Packard's premier chief executive and president for more than 32 years, the 1952 Pan American is the latest addition to the automotive collection at the Detroit Historical Museum. Donated by former Detroiter J. Bell Moran now living in Palm Beach, Florida, the car will be loaned for the grand opening of the new National Packard Museum in Packard's birthplace, Warren, Ohio, where it will remain on display through 1999, Packard's centennial celebration year.

*T*o test the waters further, Packard management approved the construction of five more Pan Americans for the show car circuit. This example made the route early in 1953. *Department of Automotive History, Detroit Historical Museums*

though financially successful, was ultimately a genuine flop. The same can be said of the mildly face-lifted carryover models of the 1949–1950 Twenty-Third Series. Packard managed to ride on its reputation and the pent-up demand for new cars in the first years of the postwar era, but as the economy settled down in the early 1950s, Packard arrived at a crossroad and made the first of several wrong turns.

In a misguided quest to offer lower-priced cars competitive with Ford, GM, and Chrysler, Packard's new president, former company treasurer Hugh Ferry, continued to dilute the model lines as had his predecessor, although he was abundantly more farsighted than Christopher and responsible for many of the achievements Packard would make after he stepped down in 1952.

The all-new Twenty-Fourth Series, introduced in 1950 as a 1951 model, improved the calendar year, and with it Packard styling, but by then East Grand had lost too much ground to the competition in the eyes of Packard loyalists. The once aristocratic Packard empire was teetering on the edge of disaster when Hugh Ferry found James J. Nance, a man he believed could steer Packard in the right direction. It took almost two years to convince Nance, who was the president of Hotpoint and one of the

highest-profile corporate executives in America, to leave the General Electric fold and accept a position with Packard. But in 1952 Ferry graciously retired, and Nance was elected president and general manager of Packard.

Jim Nance had a background in sales and marketing, not automobiles, and as such, his perspective was untarnished by the realities of the automotive industry. Unfortunately, this also meant that he had no understanding of the intractable costs of automobile production, many of which could not be changed, and others which increased in scale each year whether or not the price of the car itself could be raised to compensate. The cost of Packard bodies built by Briggs was one of them. Coachwork, which had long been East Grand's strong suit, would prove to be the auto maker's Achilles' heel in the coming years.

In less than a year, Nance had begun a complete overhaul of Packard, including executive restructuring and the early "retirement" of those he felt were no longer useful to the company's future. He brought in some of his executive staff from Hotpoint to fill key positions, thus creating his own inner sanctum at Packard. Each step in Nance's plan for the company's resuscitation was methodically carried out. The wheels of change within Packard ran slowly, but steadily. Regarding his managerial style, Nance told a *Newsweek* reporter, "I was what you might call a cautious man in a hurry."[1]

Beginning with the Twenty-Sixth Series, Nance changed the system in which models were designated. Each Packard model was given a distinctive name and offered in only one body style. This was the marketing man in Nance. He was employing a psychologically based strategy that had worked in the appliance business. First, products with names were more easily identified, and second, they allowed an immediate hierarchy to be established within the Packard line that provided a mental picture to form as each model name was mentioned.

The new designations were Mayfair, Caribbean, Packard Convertible, Cavalier, Patrician, Formal Sedan, Corporate Limousine, and Executive Sedan. The Patrician was for the man who had position. The Cavalier was for the man on the way up. The Convertible was for the playboy, and the Mayfair for the man whose wife wouldn't let him be a playboy.[2]

The medium-priced Clipper models were designated as Clipper, Clipper DeLuxe, and Clipper Sportster, the latter being a two-door sports coupe. Under Nance, Packard now had a dozen models with

13 body styles, better than double the number of choices offered in 1952.

The all-new 1953 model line was the first publicly recognized achievement under Nance, spearheaded by the luxurious, limited-production Caribbean, a car that brought back all the magic of Packard's luxury car image, combined with fresh, innovative styling, and exclusivity.

The Caribbean had its styling rooted in the 1952 Packard Pan American show car, which had been championed by Nance's predecessor, Hugh Ferry. Designed by Richard Arbib of the Henney Motor Company in Freeport, Illinois, the Pan American was adapted from a leftover 1951 production Packard convertible. The construction contract was awarded February 15, 1952, on condition that the car be ready for the New York International Motor Sports Show little more than a month away. Arbib, a former GM stylist who had worked under Bill Mitchell, pushed

*T*he Packard convertible was the basis for the custom-built Caribbeans. The differences between this 1952 model and the Ionia-built Caribbeans is evident from the hood back. *Department of Automotive History, Detroit Historical Museums*

*P*ackard contracted with the Mitchell-Bentley Company of Ionia, Michigan, to convert 750 standard Packard convertibles into a limited run of "personal sports cars" introduced as the Caribbean in 1953.

137

The body styling for the 1951 models, penned by John Reinhart, was the most alluring that East Grand had come up with since the Darrin-designed 1941 Clipper. The bold shape of the grille redefined the Packard front end, establishing a look that would last until 1954. In October 1950, the 1951 Packard was named by the Society of Motion Picture Art Directors as "the most beautiful car of the year . . . the car which embodies the most advanced concepts of automotive styling." *National Automotive History Collection, Detroit Public Library*

*I*n the early 1950s, American cars were all three-box designs. Packard chose to use well-rounded contours for its 1951 models and one of the earliest wraparound rear windows. Pictured is a 1951 Model 300 touring sedan. *Department of Automotive History, Detroit Historical Museums*

*T*he 1951 models breathed new life into Packard styling. The all-new designs were carried over into 1952 for the Twenty-Fifth Series. In addition, Packard had the intermediate-priced Mayfair models and convertible, introduced in March 1951. Pictured from front to rear, the 1951 Patrician 400, the 300 touring sedan, and 200 touring sedan. *Department of Automotive History, Detroit Historical Museums*

the Henney design team around the clock to meet the March 29 deadline. The car had to have a unique look, thus Arbib had the body sectioned 4 inches to provide a lower silhouette; the windshield, radiator, steering column, and suspension were also lowered to contribute a ground-hugging effect. Intended to appear as a "sports car," although on a somewhat larger scale, the rear seat was removed and the area enclosed with a metal tonneau cover. A functional air scoop was added to the hood, and a trendy continental kit mounted for the spare tire.

The Pan American was the hit of the New York show. Dealers and customers flooded East Grand with requests for a production version, but to build such a car for sale was virtually impossible. It was too expensive to manufacture, its low-slung suspension impractical for everyday use, and since it was only a show car, there had been no provision for a convertible top, which would have required even more prohibitive costs for development and tooling. The car had, however, stirred public interest and sales momentum that Packard could ill afford to lose. To test the waters further, management approved the construction of five more Pan Americans for the show car circuit.

The original car was returned to the factory styling department, where it underwent changes that dramatically altered its appearance. An "egg-crate" inner grille pattern was substituted for the original heavy horizontal bar scheme. Round taillights were retained, but chrome fin moldings came off the rear fenders. Wire wheels were replaced with standard wheels and turbine-type covers featuring a large chrome and cloisonné center medallion. The last major change was an "update" to reflect the newly styled 1955 Packards, adding distinctive Richard Teague–designed cathedral taillights with integrated exhaust port bumpers and a front fender canted extension above the headlights. A 1955 instrument panel, steering column, and front bumper completed the changes.

The Macauley family owned the original Pan American for about 20 years, and Edward Macauley's widow, Marge, personalized it with a large script *M* on the hood center and added stunning brass door medallions with her initials set in rubies within a circle of diamonds. The car is now part of the automotive collection at the Detroit Historical Museum.

Public response to the Pan Americans was the same everywhere they appeared, and by spring 1952,

Nance had authorized a production version to be based on the upcoming 1953 convertible designed by Packard's new chief stylist Dick Teague. Like the show car, this too, would have to be a rush job ready for debut in less than a year. Packard contracted with the Mitchell-Bentley Company of Ionia, Michigan, to convert 750 standard Packard convertibles into a limited-run of "personal sports cars" introduced as the Caribbean in 1953, and followed in 1954 by another 400 units of similar, though more luxurious, design.

The Caribbean name was continued in 1955 and 1956, the last two years of true Packard production, but the cars were standard-body convertibles with no resemblance to either the Pan American or earlier Caribbeans.

By 1954, Nance had upgraded the Packard line with more luxurious and expensive models to compete with Cadillac and Lincoln and expanded the Clipper series to compete against lower-priced cars from GM and Chrysler. Nance's efforts to rebuild Packard seemed to be working, and then everything began to crumble. Profits fell late in 1953, as did sales after credit tightened and banks began demanding larger down-payments on car loans. At the same time, Ford and GM were battling it out to see who could produce the most cars. On any given day, Ford and Chevrolet assembly lines were turning out more cars than Packard could produce in an entire month. Given Packard's share of the market, less than 3 percent of new car sales in the early 1950s, East Grand was producing more than enough cars.

The real undermining of the Packard empire began in December 1953, when Briggs, Packard's

The 1953 Twenty-Sixth Series was highlighted by the Caribbean, Model 2631, powered by the venerable straight eight, developing 180 horsepower. Built on a 122-inch wheelbase, the Caribbean was listed in 1953 as "Convertible Sports Car." Pictured to the left of the Caribbean is the Model 2611 Clipper DeLuxe touring sedan, powered by the 160-horsepower eight-cylinder engine. *National Automotive History Collection, Detroit Public Library*

The senior model in 1953 was the Patrician, built on a 127-inch-wheelbase chassis and equipped with the 180-horsepower engine. Pictured is a Model 2606 touring sedan. *National Automotive History Collection, Detroit Public Library*

principal coachbuilder, sold out to Chrysler. Nance was faced with a number of possibilities. These included re-establishing the in-house facility at East Grand to manufacture its own shells, contracting bodies from the handful of remaining independent coachbuilders, a financially unfeasible alternative, or purchasing bodies from Chrysler, an even more distasteful prospect, which Chrysler rejected anyway, telling Nance that Briggs would only produce Packard bodies for the 1954 model year. After that, Packard would have to find someone else. In the midst of everything, Nance now had to figure out how Packard would build bodies for its 1955 models. This provoked him to reconsider something he had discussed with Nash-Kelvinator president and fellow appliance maker George Mason prior to assuming the Packard helm — merging Packard with another company.

On the advice of his vice president of manufacturing, Ray Powers, however, Nance formulated another alternative: to abandon the old body factory at East Grand, which was an antiquated multistory affair, in favor of leasing the vacant Briggs building on Conner Avenue from Chrysler and using it to set up a new assembly line. It was a difficult decision, and the Packard board voted to take Nance's advice, moving

the entire operation to Conner Avenue in time to begin production of 1955 models. It was the fatal shot, and Jim Nance was left holding the smoking gun.

While the Briggs debacle was taking shape, Nance was seriously pursuing the idea of a merger. The most likely candidate was Studebaker, followed by a consolidation with Mason's companies giving the resulting conglomerate a product line that would level the playing field with GM, Ford, and Chrysler. And had that happened, there would probably still be Packards, Studebakers, and Hudsons on the road today. The auto industry would have been far more diversified and competitive in the coming years, and better able to respond to the changing market trends that toppled Detroit's domination of the American road in the 1970s, opening the door for Japanese imports. Indeed, it would be a different world today had Nance and Mason succeeded.

The concept was certainly sound. William C. Durant created General Motors by bringing four

*P*ackard dealership in 1954 displaying new models. *Department of Automotive History, Detroit Historical Museums*

One of the few highlights in Packard's declining years was the Panther-Daytona concept car, a running prototype built to compete in the Speed Week competition at Daytona Beach, Florida, in 1954. The car was designed by Packard chief stylist Dick Teague, seated behind the wheel. Behind the car are Packard director of design Ed Macauley (left) and executive engineer Bill Graves. The car was driven at Daytona by Indy race driver Dick Rathman, who clocked 110.9 miles per hour on the sand. Not satisfied with the car's performance, he made an "unofficial" run streaking through the traps at 131 miles per hour.

independent auto makers together under a single banner in the formative years of the American automotive industry. This was the rationale behind a proposal formulated by Mason at Nash-Kelvinator in Kenosha, Wisconsin. Nash would merge with Hudson, creating American Motors Corporation, and then Packard and Studebaker would come in, giving the combined Wisconsin-Indiana-Detroit conglomerate a complete line of cars from trendsetting compacts to full-sized luxury cars, plus the prestige of the Hudson and Packard passenger cars and Studebaker's popular line of trucks.

In theory it would have worked, but as Nance later discovered, trying to control two companies in different states—with different management techniques and employee attitudes, different unions and pay scales, and conflicting marketing and production methods—was a recipe for corporate chaos. Had the AMC merger taken place, however, the results might well have been different with Nash and Mason in the equation.

During the 1930s, Nash had held a steady place in American car production and in 1937 merged with the Kelvinator Corporation, the well-known maker of refrigerators. This came about because company founder Charles Nash wanted George Mason as his executive vice president and to get Mason he had to buy Kelvinator. Mason was no stranger to the auto business, having been with Studebaker, Dodge, and Chrysler before becoming president of Kelvinator in 1928. With Mason's arrival, Nash felt he could begin to slow down and at

age 74 went into semi-retirement, leaving the operation of Nash-Kelvinator to Mason.

Nash started the 1950s in excellent financial shape, having been one of the first American auto makers back in production after the war in 1945, winning third place in sales behind Ford and Chevrolet. Of course, once the Big Three got rolling, Nash quickly tumbled back to 11th place. Even so, profits were high, and the company recorded an $18 million profit in 1947.

When Charlie Nash passed away in 1948, at the age of 84, Mason moved up the corporate ladder and appointed as his right-hand man George Romney (in later years governor of Michigan and a presidential candidate). Under Mason, Nash broke new ground in several areas, including the importing of foreign cars built jointly by Nash, British auto maker Donald Healey, and Italian coachbuilder Battista "Pinin" Farina. The larger Nashes also had been styled by Pinin Farina, giving the American cars a more European flavor.

Mason's general philosophy was to offer buyers automobiles that the Detroit establishment did not, and in 1950 he broke new ground with the Rambler, a compact car built on a short 100-inch wheelbase and powered by an economical 85-horsepower six-cylinder engine.

Despite an interesting product line, Nash soon found itself in the same shape as other independent auto makers who were losing sales to GM, Ford, and Chrysler faster than they could calculate it. By early 1953, the market share of the independent car makers had declined from 18.6 percent in 1946 to less than 5 percent, at which point reasoned Mason, "If you can't beat them, join them." He merged Nash with Hudson, forming American Motors Corporation in January 1954, at the time the biggest merger in American automotive history.

Although it was never directly discussed by Mason and Nance after Nance became president of Packard, the subsequent consolidation of Packard and Studebaker appeared sound. As Nance would discover all too late, unlike Nash and Hudson, Studebaker was a company living off reflected light by 1954.

In the late 1940s and very early 1950s, Studebaker had been a force to be reckoned with. Innovative and highly competitive, the South Bend, Indiana, company brought in the best engineers and designers available to create the first all-new postwar models sold in the United States.

Among a handful of tricks to make the cars more attractive to customers was the triple paint scheme, an idea that probably did more harm than good, as the dictates of good taste seemed to decline proportionately with the number of color combinations available.

At Studebaker's design helm was internationally renowned stylist Raymond Loewy, and a staff headed by Virgil Exner, legendary Duesenberg stylist Gordon Buehrig, and John Reinhart, who had been with Packard before.

Loewy's first postwar design, introduced in 1946, gave way to an all-new model in 1950 with a controversial look that to this day is still the subject of debate. It was either one of the most innovative designs of the era, or one of the ugliest. After Reinhart and Buehrig moved on to Ford and Exner to Chrysler, Loewy set about designing American cars with a European flair. The 1953 Studebakers were stunning. The automotive press heaped superlatives on the new models, comparing them in importance with the first Lincoln Continental and the Cord 810. General Motors, Ford, and Chrysler may have been bigger, but for this one brief moment in history the little company from Indiana was stealing all the press and giving Detroit something to think about.

Unfortunately, against the Motor City's big guns, Studebaker could not build a competitively priced car. Studebakers were too expensive, and the company's old-fashioned way of doing business left deal-

ers with no margin to price their cars competitively against Ford, Chevrolet, and Dodge models. With what amounted to the best cars Studebaker had built in years, and perhaps the best American-made cars of the early 1950s, Studebaker found itself facing legions of disgruntled dealers and ledger pages underscored in red ink. By the end of 1953, Studebaker seemed an ideal candidate for a merger.

Nance saw the company in a different light, one with a long-established reputation like Packard's, and indeed Studebaker was one of the country's oldest, having emerged out of the Studebaker family's renowned wagon-making business in the late 1800s. South Bend also provided something Nance desperately needed: body manufacturing facilities. The combined Studebaker-Packard resources would have factories in Detroit; Utica (Packard's newest); South Bend; Los Angeles; New Brunswick; New Jersey; Hamilton, Ontario; and Mexico City.

In the best of all possible worlds, Packard would be viewed as Studebaker's rescuer, and Nance the hero. It was, as he later lamented, "a shotgun wedding," and in the rush to merge, neither Packard nor Studebaker had formally reviewed its actual sales figures. For Packard,

James J. Nance had yet to lose confidence in his ability to save Packard through the merger with Studebaker, and despite all of the pitfalls that frustrated his progress in 1955, he was still optimistic about the coming year and the improved 1956 models. Sadly, his enthusiasm did not spread to the buying public. *Department of Automotive History, Detroit Historical Museums*

"*N*othing Can Stop Us Now" was the theme of Nance's October 1955 meeting to launch the 1956 Packard line. The banquet was held at the Fairmont Hotel in San Francisco. Among the listeners seated at the speaker's table were legendary auto dealer Earle C. Anthony (far left), one of Nance's confidants and advisors; LeRoy Spencer, Pacific divisional manager; Robert J. Laughna, Packard vice president and general manager, Packard-Clipper Division; and George Wagner, executive vice president and general manager of Earle C. Anthony Inc. *Department of Automotive History, Detroit Historical Museums*

this was of little consequence. The numbers were always fairly consistent. Studebaker, on the other hand, had misjudged its break-even point by 73 percent, or a difference of around 120,000 more cars than the company could sell. This news was not well received in the Packard boardroom. There was, however, still the possibility of consolidation with American Motors, an arrangement that would have made Billy Durant proud, had George Mason not died suddenly in 1954. Nance was lost.

Mason's successor, George Romney, was not a big James Nance fan, and now that he was in the driver's seat, Romney had no interest in pursuing any plan to combine American Motors with the newly merged Studebaker-Packard concern, which he viewed as an amalgamation of two foundering companies. In one respect, Romney was dead right. Studebaker was in big trouble, and East Grand was saddled with a financially challenged South Bend, Indiana, operation, losing money faster than Packard could make it up.

Were this not enough, Packard lost a large percentage of its defense contracts at the end of the Korean conflict in July 1953, and Studebaker lost all of its government business, a combined total of roughly $329 million from January 1953 to June 1954. The majority of new government contracts were funneled to General Motors, a politically driven decision, and some believe a quite deliberate one, that broke Studebaker-Packard's back. Nance was banking on profits from Pentagon contracts to build jet and marine engines in 1953, which would help finance retooling for the 1955 model year. It was a catastrophic loss, but the final blow really came from within. It was the Briggs building on Conner Avenue.

The new assembly plant was ill-suited for mass production, and it took until late 1955 to get all the bugs worked out. Cars were coming off the line with such poor build quality that dealers had to make repairs before they could sell them. There were missing parts; loose wires; poorly fitting doors; nonfunctioning radios, clocks, and wind-

Following the October 25, 1955, dinner at the Fairmont Hotel in San Francisco, Packard dealers and their wives were treated to a private showing of 1956 models, including the new Caribbean hardtop. *Department of Automotive History, Detroit Historical Museums*

The Packard dealer meeting in October 1955 included a look at the new 1956 Packard chassis with Torsion Level Ride, later acclaimed by the automotive press as one of the best suspension systems to emerge from Detroit in years. *Department of Automotive History, Detroit Historical Museums*

The Packard Four Hundred was at the top of the model line in 1956. The Torsion Level Ride was the car's most attractive unseen feature, prominently displayed in advertising and brochures. *National Automotive History Collection, Detroit Public Library*

Packard dealers were easy to spot at this 1956 debut; they're the ones in the white cowboy hats. Little did anyone realize this was to be the last year Packard would be a stand-alone design. The end of the road had been reached, but no one saw the sign. Maybe the hats were blocking their vision.
Department of Automotive History, Detroit Historical Museums

shield wipers; and generally inferior quality on every aspect of the automobiles.

In the face of unprecedented warranty repairs, Packard posted a loss of $30 million in 1955 on the sale of 69,667 cars. Nance, ever the optimist, kicked off the annual meeting with the slogan, "Nothing can stop us now!" In truth, it should have been, "We have met the enemy, and he is us."

Studebaker-Packard was a house of cards about to collapse, yet in spite of political machinations

from Secretary of Defense Wilson and the Pentagon chiefs, the turmoil at Conner Avenue, and a seemingly irreversible flow of red ink, Nance and the men of Packard managed to produce beautifully styled cars for 1956 loaded with innovative new features.

The groundwork for the 1956 models had been laid with the troubled 1955 cars, which had introduced the company's first V-8 engines, available in either 327- or 352-cubic-inch displacements, a revised dual-range automatic transmission, and Tor-

*I*t was the best car in Packard's postwar history, but to a public whose confidence in the products had been uprooted by years of unpopular designs, shoddy construction, and unprecedented warranty repairs, the stunning new 1956 Packards were barely able to generate enough sales to justify keeping the assembly lines running. The cars featured Ultramatic, with a push-button shifter to the right of the steering column, a beautifully upholstered and designed interior, and optional air conditioning.

sion Level Ride suspension, achievements that should have been impossible given Packard's financial dilemma.

Motor Trend's review of the 1955 Packards said, "Everything else dims by comparison with ride. . . ." Car Life proclaimed Torsion Level Ride as ". . . a great contribution to the world's motoring industry. Not only is the 1955 Packard safer than many of its contemporaries, but it is much more comfortable." Floyd Clymer Books, which published a variety of automotive and general interest publications,

applauded the car's ability to go into a turn at speed, with the body remaining almost perfectly level.

With such glowing reviews, Packard should have had a banner year in 1955, but the quality of the cars was killing sales by the score. Packard was streaming down the road to extinction at full throttle. By the time 1956 models were rolling out the door, Conner Avenue was building the best Packards in more than a decade, but it was too little, too late. The buying public had lost confidence. For the first two months of the year, auto industry sales fell 17 percent due to tighter credit on new car

loans and a disproportionate carryover of unsold 1955 models, which were nearly twice the annual level. Studebaker sales had dropped by 23 percent for the period ending in February 1956, and Packard deliveries had plummeted a staggering 67 percent.

By the end of the first quarter of 1956, it was clear that Studebaker-Packard would not survive the year unless drastic steps were taken. Nance started cutting production and operations at both companies, laying off workers, and using all available credit to keep the company afloat. Proposals to merge with Ford, General Motors, and Chrysler had all been turned down by the auto makers, as had a final attempt at consolidating with American Motors. The Packard board was now considering the option of selling the company to any of several possible suitors, including International Harvester, General Dynamics, Massey-Harris, or defense contractor Curtiss-Wright. Still there were no takers, and the reality of liquidation was at hand. A prospect no one on the Packard board wanted to contemplate. The inevitable was at hand when Curtiss-Wright President Roy T. Hurley intervened in the spring of 1956.

Neither fish nor fowl. It was unofficially dubbed the "Packardbaker," South Bend's hybrid 1958 four-door sedan combining a long, low Studebaker silhouette with Packard trademark trim. A long, graceful sweep of gold anodized aluminum accentuated the flowing lines of the new car. Power brakes and automatic transmission were standard equipment on all Packards.
National Automotive History Collection, Detroit Public Library

After protracted negotiations with the Packard board of directors, close-to-the-vest dealing in Washington to secure defense contracts for Studebaker-Packard under the auspices of Curtiss-Wright, and the spin-off of Studebaker-Packard's defense subsidiary Utica-Bend as a wholly owned subsidiary of Curtiss-Wright, Studebaker-Packard got a much needed infusion of working capital and a chance at survival. It would, however, be at the cost of Packard. Hurley was now the power behind the throne. On July 25, 1956, the same day James J. Nance announced his resignation, it was decided Packard production would be moved to Studebaker's South Bend, Indiana, headquarters. The glory days at East Grand Boulevard were over.

Nance's departure hastened the resignation of other former Packard managers and soon most of the Old Guard were gone. Nance landed at Ford Motor Company as vice president of marketing and then vice president of the new Mercury, Edsel, Lincoln Division,

which, through no fault of Nance's, failed within the year leading to his resignation from Ford. He became president of the Central National Bank in Cleveland, Ohio, and later its chairman and CEO. In 1984 James J. Nance died at his summer home in Bellaire, Michigan, at age 83. He forever bore the stigma as the man who ruined Packard, but as history has shown, he was just one of the pawns in a much larger game.

After Nance's departure in 1956, Studebaker-Packard came under the direction of Studebaker boss Harold Churchill, who answered to Hurley at Curtiss-Wright. His first order of business was preserving the Packard name, at least temporarily, in as much as there were still Packard dealers. For a mere $1 million in tooling, Studebaker-Packard was able to fudge the design of Studebaker models and hang enough Packard trim on them to create the illusion of a new Packard line for 1957. But for all intents and purposes,

Packard had ceased to exist. Studebaker had a deal with Daimler-Benz to begin marketing Mercedes in May, giving Studebaker-Packard dealers a high-dollar luxury car to sell in addition to Studebakers and "Packardbakers." In 1958, the Packard name appeared on a new model, the Packard Hawk, a sportier version of the Studebaker Hawk; however, Packard sales continued to decline, and when the 1959 models arrived, Packards were nowhere to be seen. The marque had quietly died in its sleep. A brief announcement was made by Studebaker-Packard in July 1958, but there was no ceremony to acknowledge the passing of a legendary marque.[3]

The *New York Times* and *Wall Street Journal* both ran articles on Packard, the *Times* noting that with Packard's demise, only 16 remained of the 2,700 nameplates that had appeared since 1893. *Business Week* headlined a story, "Ask the Man Who Owned One," and compared the fall of Nash, Hudson, Willys, Kaiser, Crosley, Frazier, and Packard to the disappearance of automobile companies in the Depression.

By the end of the 1950s, one of the greatest companies in the history of the automobile in America arrived at the final crossroad and vanished silently with those who had gone before and never returned.

*B*uilt on the Studebaker's 120-inch-wheelbase chassis and powered by an extremely robust supercharged 275-horsepower, 289-cubic-inch V-8 engine, the Hawk was a poorly proportioned car with only the Packard name and bottom-feeding catfish grille to distinguish it from a Studebaker. The 1958 Packard Hawk was a sorrowful end to East Grand's legacy.

*P*ackard's high profile and individual identity were practically nonexistent when this advertisement from Studebaker-Packard Corporation appeared in magazines in 1956.

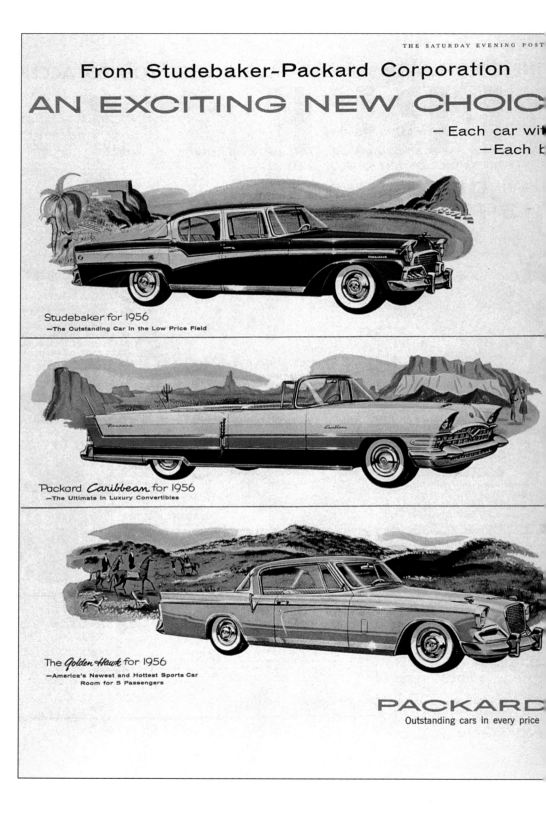

N EVERY PRICE CLASS

sonality unmistakably its own

the company that brings you the <u>newest</u> advances <u>first</u>!

Packard for 1956
—Setting New Standards in Fine Cars

Clipper for 1956
—America's Finest Medium Price Car—
Built by Packard Craftsmen

THE BOLD NEW IDEA

Puts you far in advance with the features of the future

At Studebaker-Packard, the *Bold New Idea* means that the
American motorist is given an exciting *new choice* of cars in every price class.
Each car possesses a *personality* of its own, the result of distinctive craftsmanship,
and each possesses *product advantages* well in advance of the industry —
the result of far-sighted engineering and the unique flexibility
·of production made possible by this young, vigorous company.

Torsion-Level Suspension makes possible *a smoother, safer
ride* through the elimination of coil and leaf springs. It is one
of the major engineering advancements recently pioneered
by Studebaker-Packard—and inspired by the *Bold New Idea*.

LIPPER · STUDEBAKER

cts of Studebaker-Packard Corporation

153

Notes

Chapter 1

1. Martin, Terry. *Packard—A History of the Motor Car and the Company*, chapter 2, "The First of the Marque."
2. Packard offered its cars with a wide range of outputs, from the standard 9-horsepower Model B to as much as 24-horsepower for the Model C.
3. President McKinley died of his wounds eight days later and Vice President Theodore Roosevelt became the 26th president of the United States.

Chapter 2

1. *Packard—A History of the Motor Car and the Company*, chapter six, "A Gentlemen's Car, Built by Gentlemen," by James J. Bradley.

Chapter 4

1. In 1924 Cadillac added four-wheel brakes to its eight-cylinder models as well; however, Packard introduced the Single Eight before Cadillac debuted its 1924 line. Cadillac had introduced the V-8 in 1915, the same year Packard announced the 1916 Twin Six.

Chapter 5

1. There were 13 factory body styles among Models 1406, 1407, and 1408, plus two catalogued LeBaron offerings for 1936, a 1407 all-weather cabriolet and 1408 all-weather town car.

Chapter 7

1. With sales of 47,855, 1929 was Packard's best year up until 1935, when sales rebounded to 52,045. The company's best prewar sales year was 1937, with total production reaching 109,518.

Chapter 8

1. Miller's record, and the "Fastest Speedway" title, would stand for 24 years, until the Monza course was built in Italy.
2. *Packard—A History of the Motor Car and the Company*, appendix II, "The Packard Proving Grounds," by Nemmo Duerksen; and *The Fall of the Packard Motor Car Company*, by James A. Ward.
3. *Packard—A History of the Motor Car and the Company*, appendix II, "The Packard Proving Grounds," by Nemmo Duerksen.
4. Ibid
5. Ibid

Chapter 9

1. ZIS, pronounced "zees," was the official state car. The initial letters stood for Z, factory; I, in honor of; and S, Stalin.
2. *Packard—A History of the Motor Car and the Company*, chapter 26, "One Guess What Name It Bears," by George Hamlin and Dwight Heinmuller.

Chapter 10

1. *Packard—A History of the Motor Car and the Company*, chapter 18, "The End Of An Era," by L. Morgan Yost.
2. The long-wheelbase DeLuxe Super Eights were essentially more affordable versions of the Custom Eight seven-passenger limousine and sedan, priced some $850 less.

Chapter 11

1. *The Fall of the Packard Motor Car Company*, by James A. Ward.
2. *The Packard 1942–1962*, by Nathaniel T. Dawes.
3. *The Fall of the Packard Motor Car Company*, by James A. Ward.

$\mathcal{B}$ibliography

Adler, Dennis. *Fifties Flashback.* Osceola, Wis.: Motorbooks International, 1996.

Dawes, Nathaniel T. *The Packard 1942–1962.* London: A. S. Barnes and Company, 1975.

Kimes, Beverly Rae, George Hamlin, and Dwight Heinmuller. *Packard— A History of the Motor Car and the Company.* Automobile Quarterly Publications, 1978.

Murphy, Russ Jr. *The Pan American.* Meadow Brook Concours d'Elegance program, 1997.

Neal, Robert J. *Packards at Speed.* Aero-Marine Publishing Company, 1995.

Pfau, Hugo. *The Coachbuilt Packard.* England: Dalton Watson, Fine Books, 1992.

Turnquist, Robert. *The Packard Story.* A. S. Barnes and Company, 1965.

Ward, James A. *The Fall of the Packard Motor Car Company.* Stanford: Stanford University Press, 1995.

Additional research by Donald Sommer, Russ Murphy Jr., the Detroit Historical Museums, and David Holls.